5/28/07

81

The
Architecture
of
Arata Isozaki

Arata Isozaki, 1977

The
Architecture
of
Arata Isozaki

Philip Drew

ICON EDITIONS

 HARPER & ROW, PUBLISHERS, New York
Cambridge, Philadelphia, San Francisco,
1817 London, Mexico City, São Paulo, Sydney

THE ARCHITECTURE OF ARATA ISOZAKI. Copyright © 1982 by Philip Drew. Copyright ©
Arata Isozaki 1978 for 'An Architecture of Quotation and Metaphor'. All rights reserved.
Printed in Great Britain. No part of this book may be used or reproduced in any manner
whatsoever without written permission except in the case of brief quotations embodied in
critical articles and reviews. For information address Harper & Row, Publishers, Inc., 10
East 53rd Street, New York, N.Y. 10022. Published simultaneously in Canada by Fitzhenry
& Whiteside Limited, Toronto.

FIRST U.S. EDITION
ISBN: 0-06-431550-9
LIBRARY OF CONGRESS CATALOGUE CARD NUMBER: 81-48061

First published in Great Britain 1982 by
Granada Publishing Limited – Technical Books Division
Frogmore, St Albans, Herts AL2 2NF
and
36 Golden Square, London W1R 4AH

82 83 84 85   10 9 8 7 6 5 4 3 2 1

Contents

To Justine

Preface

Both within Japan and outside it Isozaki's position as a leading designer and proponent of counter-Modern ideas is founded on his intelligence and sensitivity to new trends and movements, and on his originality in finding solutions to the artistic problems which beset world architecture from the 1960s on. The side of Isozaki's architecture which interests me in particular is its affinity with Mannerism, for one detects in the kindred relations between his architecture and sixteenth century Italian Mannerism, an unmistakable family likeness.

In less than half a century architecture has moved away from the doctrine of Functionalism, which sought to make content the controlling factor in architectural form, to a new Formalism, which in effect seeks to reverse the established relationship of form and content exemplified by Early Modern architecture. It comes as no surprise therefore to discover that Isozaki is inspired less by function than by other works of architecture, for his work is best viewed as quintessential architecture.

In many ways Isozaki's values are the very antithesis of Modern architecture, and his work may therefore be interpreted in a wider historical and cultural frame as providing a clear indication of the character and aims of the counter-Modern reaction. The evidence for such a reaction in terms of criticism and polemics and design is conspicuous after 1960. For many of the younger post-Second World War architects it seemed that Modern architecture was too one-sided, and that within the framework of its exclusive, reductive aims, all the problems had been solved. It seemed to them, that while they accepted the orthodox tenets of Modernism there was nothing left for them to accomplish. Isozaki was active, and in no small measure his importance derives from his drive to establish an aesthetic to replace Modern architecture.

The view I wish to offer of Isozaki, as distinct from Charles Jencks's didactic interpretation of post-Modern in terms of the semiotic analogy, is of Isozaki as a type of Mannerist reacting to Modern architecture in much the same way that a Raphael, Giulio Romano, or Palladio reacted to the High

Renaissance. Such a comparison is illuminating for two reasons; first, one is confronted by the historical circumstances in which a younger generation seeking new avenues of expression and feeling itself overwhelmed by the completeness of their predecessor's achievements, were driven to seek a new style of their own creation, and second, both the Renaissance and Modern architecture evolved a classical aesthetic with a single focus. Both sixteenth century Italian Mannerism and later on post-Modern architecture in the 1970s are essentially anti-classical styles which seek to express a view of life as comprising multiple focii, for the essence of Mannerism is to be found in the tension between, and the union of, irreconcilable opposites. Mannerism, as this suggests, was not simply an anti-classical aesthetic; it was much more than that, and sought to structure its forms according to the principle of contrasting pairs and invoked duality, for life was conceived as complex, contradictory, and essentially ambiguous. The values expressed by Late Modern, and described by Robert Venturi, consciously recognised Mannerist sources, as if to confirm the Mannerist inspiration of the anti-Modern ideas.

Isozaki's architecture is the outcome of a dialectical response to Modern architecture, which is to say that his work is based upon the inversion and debasement of its forms. He rejects such classical principles of organisation from Modern architecture as spatial continuity, completeness of form, integration of technology and expression, identity of inside and outside, and suppression of applied decoration, and insisted instead on heterogeneous space, fragmented and incomplete form, debasement of the skeleton, discontinuity and discordance of parts, and rehabilitation of decoration.

The interpretation here offered is of Isozaki as something of a Mannerist, but there is much else in his architecture besides, as disclosed in analysis of the significance of the sacred 'Pillar of Heaven', the beam, the cube, and the cylinder. With regard to style there have been repeated shifts from one phase to the next, beginning with Brutalist megaforms which were succeeded by a quasi-Mannerist aesthetic. By the mid-1970s Neo-Classicism increasingly featured in his work, then in 1980 his architecture began to look less Neo-Classical and more strictly classical in its appearance.

It is evident from the stylistic shifts in Isozaki's architecture over the decade of the 1970s that architecture in general lacked any single principle which would assure continuity. These continual shifts of style and experimentation suggest that contemporary architecture was less original and much more dependant on earlier traditional stylistic precedent than previously – a condition reflected in the work of Isozaki. Under the circumstances, no clear direction emerged from the welter of eclecticism, which offered a degree of coherence and stability. Isozaki exemplifies the changing nature of contemporary architecture with its repeated shifts in style. He remains nevertheless the quintessential architect and for this reason alone, if for no other, deserves to be widely recognised and his work well appreciated, both within and outside Japan.

Acknowledgements

In 1978 when I visited Japan for a second time it was apparent that Arata Isozaki had become – that is since my first visit in 1967 – the foremost creative personality in Japanese architecture. I gratefully acknowledge his generous help in arranging for me to visit his buildings, in answering my numerous queries, and in arranging to have the photographs made which appear in this book. What impressed me most about Isozaki was his extraordinary energy, intelligence, and concentration, he seemed to take in everything and to be intensely focussed as an individual – without becoming in the least less human as a person, for he remains in my memory a modest, informal, even vulnerable man. I willingly confess to having fallen under the spell of his beautiful charming wife, Aiko Miyawaki; to Aiko and Arata my sincere thanks for your hospitality and kindness.

I am indebted to Toshio Nakamura of *Architecture and Urbanism* for those timeless afternoons in which we talked of Japanese architecture, Arata Isozaki, and much else besides. In no small measure you sharpened my thoughts on Arata's work and helped to relate his achievement to the more general patterns of Japanese architecture. To those other Japanese architects who talked to me and opened their minds I am most grateful; in particular, Kisho Kurokawa, Fumihiko Maki, Kiyonori Kikutake, Kazuo Shinohara, Minoru Takeyama, Toyoo Ito, Takefumi Aida, Monta Mozuna and Hiromi Fujii, I wish to express my gratitude.

The opportunity to visit Japan, the U.S.A., and Italy to study Mannerism, from which this analysis of Isozaki's architecture flowed, was made possible by a study leave grant from the University of Newcastle. It was a pleasure to meet Dennis Sharp and assist in the development of the architecture series for Granada, I am grateful to John Thackara for supporting my proposal, and to his successor Julia Burden, for her assiduous attention to detail and her efforts in overcoming the various obstacles which presented themselves from time to time. The manuscript was typed in draft by my mother, Ivy Drew, and the final typing by Sandra Barrowcliff, Sandra Carlyon, Jan Taylor and Christine Hills.

The author would like to thank the following for illustrations used in this book:

Bibliotheque Nationale, Paris (Fig. 65); Phyllis Dearborn Massar (Fig. 70); Geijutsu-Sincho (photographer Akio Nonaka) (Fig. 2); Kenichi Hoshino (*frontispiece*); Yasuhiro Ishimoto (Figs 16, 19, 21, 37, 54, 71*a*, 73*b*, 80, 86, 88, 89, 91, 92, 98, 113, 115, 116, 117, 119, 147, 148 and 149); *The Japan Architect* (photographer Masao Arai) (Figs 5, 10, 12, 15, 30, 35, 38, 47, 59*b*, 60, 68, 95, 96, 97, 109, 114, 120, 122, 123, 124, 135, 136, 137, 138, 140, 141, 142, 143, 144 and 145); *The Japan Architect* (photographer Taisuke Ogawa) (Figs 7, 31, 100, 101 and 106); Kawasumi Architectural Photograph Office (Fig. 28); Tom Kelley (Fig. 14); Kiyonori Kikutake (Fig. 6); Kunsthistorisches Museum, Vienna (Fig. 53); Osamu Murai (Figs 40 and 41); Tomio Ohashi (Figs 62, 126, 127, 128, 129 and 130); Retoria (photographer Yukio Futagawa) (Figs 9, 32*a*, 33*a*, 59*a*, 78, 81, 83, 84 and 103); Retoria (photographer Toshiharu Kitajima) (Figs 158 and 160); Retoria (photographer Yoshio Takase) (Figs 25*a*, 63*a*, 154, 155, 156, and 161); Oksuji Seiji (Fig. 104); Shokoku-sha Publishing Co. Inc. (Figs 111 and 134): Hiroaki Tanaka (Fig. 107), Tretyakov Gallery Moscow (Fig. 39); Uffizi Gallery, Florence (Fig. 11); Shuji Yamada (Figs 69, 75, 76, 77, 132, 133, 151*a*, 151*b* and 152); Hajime Yatsuka (Fig. 57). The line drawings are reproduced courtesy of Arata Isozaki and Associates.

The Publishers would like to thank Dennis Sharp for his work as Advisory Editor of this book.

I
Relations

Between Japan and the West

Arata Isozaki was born in the city of Oita on the north coast of the island of Kyushu on 23rd July 1931, and it is there that many of his projects were built. Like Kenzo Tange, who was born at Imabari, a village on the nearby island of Shikoku, Isozaki grew up in a small provincial centre far from Tokyo. Thus, although Isozaki has spent much of his adult life in Tokyo, the bulk of his architecture is located in three cities in Kyushu. Excluding houses, by 1980, Isozaki had completed eight projects in Oita, three in Fukuoka, three in Kitakyushu, and another in Saga. By contrast, only three major works of note were carried out in centres outside Kyushu.

Kyushu influenced Isozaki's development in other more subtle ways, for it is not too fanciful to detect in his career some of those southern traits which in the past have set its people apart from northern Japanese. Some part of Isozaki's independence of mind, rebelliousness, openness to Western influences, and conservative attachment to ancient Japanese archetypes comes from this southern personality, for the inhabitants of Kyushu are notably more extroverted and lively than their northern counterparts.

The pivotal geographical location of Kyushu, moored to the southern tip of the main island, Honshu, directly opposite the great peninsula of Korea, with its west coast facing China, has been crucial in assuring Kyushu a central place in the history of Japanese civilisation. Westerners may be excused for thinking of Kyushu as a remote, possibly backward island, peopled by easy-going Japanese more akin to Pacific islanders than the industrious citizenry of Tokyo or Osaka. Such a view of Kyushu though understandable since importance is equated with proximity to the main centres of government and commerce, ignores the pivotal location of Kyushu, lying between and connecting the historic centres of Japanese civilisation with China. In the past Kyushu served as the front door and quarantine station for the Japanese nation in contacts with China, and later, it facilitated the development of trade and cultural relations with the West. The remoteness of Kyushu enabled the central government to isolate, and thereby, to control, the introduction of new knowledge and technology from outside Japan.

From the earliest times the movement of peoples into Japan proceeded by way of Kyushu over the Inland Sea to central Japan, or via western Honshu to Izumo. The Yamato people, or rather tribe, who subdued central Japan were descendants of Kyushu immigrants. According to legend their ancestor, the god Ninigi-no-Mikoto, a grandson of the sun-goddess Amaterasu, descended upon Mount Takachiko in Kyushu.

In the development of cultural and trade contacts with China, Kyushu was of singular importance. The approach of the Portuguese to Japan in the sixteenth century was from the south, and it was to Kyushu that they came bringing Christianity and the smooth bore musket. For this reason, Kyushu, so remote from the centres of political power, yet so exposed to foreign contacts, has played a crucial role in the introduction of new knowledge, technology, and culture to a hermetic Japan. The exposure of Kyushu to powerful new influences and technology from China and the West, combined with its distance from the capital meant that any rebellion was difficult and costly to put down. These factors encouraged a degree of independence and progressive attitudes which have at times flared into open rebellion.

The specialised role of Kyushu in Japanese history – its exposure to new cultural influences, coupled with its remoteness and independence – throws some light on the spiritual climate of Isozaki's architecture and may go some way in explaining his appetite for Western architecture, his independence of mind, and his rebelliousness. Isozaki's capacity for absorbing Western architectural motifs is unmatched by his contemporaries. Moreover it is associated with a degree of independence and defiance which is unusual for a Japanese.

Notwithstanding the impression created by the luxuriance of Western stylistic motifs and underlying Mannerism, a structural analysis of Isozaki's architectural forms discloses an unsuspected, and wholly consistent reiteration of three types derived from the ancient 'sacred pillar'. Having secured a Japanese identity for his architectural form by a return to the symbolism of the 'sacred pillar' Isozaki is free to pursue Western motifs. In this regard, the hypertrophic amplification of traditional Japanese carpentry in his megaskeletal form type, and the accompanying hollowing out of the beams to create interior space, is suggestive of the extensive use of bamboo in the *minka** houses of southern Kyushu. The hollow tubular structure of bamboo is recalled in the powerful square beams of the Oita Prefectural Library, 1966.

Inasmuch as Isozaki is a prolific essayist and writer much given to explaining his architecture, he exemplifies the Mannerist awareness so prevalent in late-Modern architecture, of how his style related to past architecture. An involvement in writing is something he shares with his father Soji, who besides following a successful career as a businessman was the leading figure in the 'Amano-gawa' (Milky Way) group of *Haiku* poets from Kyushu. Soji Isozaki had studied law as a young man at Shanghai Dobun Academy which was founded by the Japanese Government as a training

---

* *Minka* refers to houses belonging to the people to distinguish them from the more pretentious residences of the ruling class in the feudal period.

college for officers who were to manage the newly acquired territories on the Asian mainland. But on witnessing Japanese militarism in action Soji Isozaki returned to Japan in despair to take over his father's business in the buying and transportation of rice. Isozaki's involvement in the creation of new meanings in architecture is consonant with his name for Arata means 'newness'.

Tradition and Originality

Once the vocabulary of Modern architecture became established and its usage was perfected a counter-tendency arose which debased the machine aesthetic of Modernism. In the absence of new technological advances requiring a fundamental reconsideration of architecture, architects were left with no greater challenge than that of manipulating the existing aesthetic. After the 1930s the Modern Movement crossed the Atlantic and as the International Style, spread around the world, becoming as it did, more varied and richer, only to lose its original symbolism, much as the Renaissance had done when it travelled north from Italy in the sixteenth century. Modern architecture did not die or even come to an end. Rather there was a progressive inversion of the aesthetic code, and a defiant negation of Modernism's aesthetic taboos. The debasement of Modernism was gradual, and although several new ideas were tried, such as megastructures, none offered a viable alternative to Modernism. This impasse led to a crisis of sensibility out of which a new strategy emerged, that of replacing the fundamentally classical aesthetic of the Modern Movement by an anti-classical Mannerist one. Modernism has survived, though diminished and with much of its vigour spent, as an austere kind of Neo-Classicism alongside and sometimes combined with a quasi-Mannerist style.

Arata Isozaki is a thoroughly Mannerist architect in an era coloured by quasi-Mannerist trends, whose work must perforce be judged by the standards of Mannerism. Therefore it is essential if a proper understanding of the nature of his architecture is to occur, that Isozaki's architecture is interpreted as part of the contemporary phenomenon of quasi-Mannerism. There is much else in his architecture besides Mannerism; especially as regards the choice of architectural motifs. Isozaki's architecture ranges over the Mannerist phases of history noted by Robert Venturi in *Complexity and Contradiction in Architecture*. The pursuit of a 'pure architecture', which implies the treatment of architecture as poetry, and the use of simple geometry, lies at the core of Isozaki's approach to architectural creation. Mannerism provides Isozaki with a number of aesthetic conventions and assures him the freedom necessary to create 'pure architecture'.

The fact that Isozaki is not as well known outside Japan as he should be considering his leading position within Japan, is less a reflection of his stature than it is a measure of the current standing of Japanese architecture. The flow of influence has been very one-sided, and is symptomatic of Japan's cultural and economic dependence on the West. In the past architectural critics were excited by the 'Japaneseness' of Japan's architecture – a factor which greatly *30* enhanced Kenzo Tange's international standing – however, the extreme

Westerness of Isozaki's recent architecture is today a disadvantage.

Contemporary Japanese architecture is unmistakably derivative, though it would be unwise to dismiss Isozaki's work, or that of his contemporaries, as offering little more than a naive and frequently distorted evocation of American or European taste. There are important differences; for one thing, Japanese architects have had exceptional opportunities to build. Consequently, even the most adventurous and experimental proposals may well be constructed.

Isozaki resisted the call by Charles Jencks to vulgarise architecture, and sought instead to purify the dialect and restore the currency to its full value. Jencks's critical prejudices are thoroughly American and his desire for a popularist architecture reflects the biases of American culture.[1] Isozaki belongs to a hierarchic, elitist society, and consequently never lost sight of the fact that popular culture is always dependent on, and derived from, the models and standards of an elite. Isozaki rejected the popularist argument offered by Jencks while taking much from Jencks's semantic theory, to the extent that this coincided with his poetic intention.

The *wakonyosai* recipe – Japanese spirit and Western knowledge – proved unsatisfactory in the nineteenth century when applied to the introduction of Western building techniques because style and technique are related.[2] A straightforward translation of *wakonyosai* would be Japanese style, Western construction, and while this was tried on occasion, it is aesthetically unsatisfactory. The *wakonyosai* goal of keeping Japanese spirit while acquiring the 'power' of Western technique is an important factor in Japanese architecture. In the meantime, the old *wakonyosai* formula has been adapted to fit new circumstances. In the nineteenth century the Japanese were forced to study Western eclectic styles in order to acquire a mastery of modern construction techniques. The formula in the nineteenth century was to fuse Western style and traditional Japanese plans; for Kunio Maekawa and Kenzo Tange, Japanization of form necessitated the imposition of a traditional Japanese expression on a Corbusian aesthetic. Isozaki has discovered yet another way, he opposes Western and Japanese motifs and so achieves an architectural dialectic which expresses the tension between Japanese and Western architectural traditions. The Tokyo-Yoyogi Olympic Stadiums by Tange in 1964 anticipated just such a shift from Japanese expression to Japanese symbolism.

Each shift from Japanese plan to Japanese expression to Japanese symbolism, has been accompanied by an incremental increase in the level of abstraction. At issue, is not whether Isozaki's architecture is Japanese, but rather how this is expressed. Using the methods of transformational grammar, Isozaki appropriated the symbolic constant of the 'pillar of heaven' in order to transform the conceptual or 'deep structure' of his architecture while simultaneously including a bewildering array of Western motifs in its 'surface structure'. Thus, in contrast to Kenzo Tange, whose expression is consciously Japanese, Isozaki's architecture is both Western and Japanese.

In so far as he employs 'conceptual fusion' brought about by 'counterlogical devices' such as metaphor and paradox Isozaki treats architecture as a kind of poetry. The linguistic analogy again came to the fore in the development of

1 The primitive hut, after Laugier
Primitivism is symptomatic of a desire to
return to fundamentals; with Isozaki it
showed itself in the revivication of the
ancient sacred pillar

2 The ancient sacred pillar is the primitive
archetype of traditional Japanese
architecture. The sacred pillars erected at
the four corners surrounding the Suwa
Shrine are renewed every seven years

3 City in the Air, 1960
In this sketch Isozaki seized on the Greek
Doric order to explore the pillar in Western
tradition

architectural theory in the 1960s, and in doing so, provided an intellectually obscure justification for architectural Mannerism. In Isozaki's case, such an appropriation of semantic theory supported his underlying poetic intention. Poetry recognises a separate aesthetic function, which may be defined as 'the use of language for the sake of linguistic artefact itself, and for no other ulterior purpose'.[3] 'Pure architecture' implies among other things the ascendency of the aesthetic function, and an architecture treated as language is treated in poetry. The linguistic analogy is invalid in so far as it offers an explanation of architectural phenoma in other than architectural terms.[4] The analysis of architecture should be free from subservience to other disciplines, including semantics. The remedy is to study relations within architecture.

Primitivism is a feature of Mannerism and is also present in Neo-Classicism. It is symptomatic of a return to fundamentals and a revivification of archetypes such as in Laugier's primitive wooden hut. The collage 'City in the Air' illustrates Isozaki's desire to return to a primitive archetype of the Doric column of ancient Greek architecture. Isozaki explored several other archetypes besides the Doric column; he revived the 'sacred column' of Shinto and bracket systems from the twelfth century Japanese Jodo-do style of the Tōdaiji which are characterised by monumental scale and primitive expression. Moreover, Isozaki simplified his forms to cubes and semi-cylinders, then enlarged their scale, so as to create an atmosphere of disturbance and unreality. Isozaki's reduction of architectural form to pure cubes and semi-cylinders introduces a second element of primitiveness. This follows on from and is directly related to the earlier megastructure movement which sought to consider problems of the city as a single structure. The change from spatial division to spatial addition is generally retrogressive and flows from a desire to return to the primitive. Such a desire is understandable as a reaction to advanced industrialism and the chaotic urbanism of Japanese cities in the 1970s.

Architecture is now much more concerned with manipulating established aesthetics than it is with the creation of something new, though it would be a mistake in a period of transition to fail to detect in all of this new and original forces. Isozaki's architecture is of international interest because he deals with universal problems which arise from the crisis of the Modern Movement. With the advent of Late Modern architecture the urgent quest for the communication of function was replaced by a new historicism. In an attack on the new historicism, which also included an early reference to 'Post-modern' architecture in 1961 Nikolaus Pevsner[5] contended that the return to historicism was occasioned by a revolt against Rationalism. Pevsner placed the beginnings of the new 'Post-modern' anti-Rationalism as early as 1938 and cited Scandinavian housing and the later work of Oud as marking the retreat from the International Style in the 1930s. What Pevsner failed to appreciate fully is that all artistic activity comprises a simultaneous interaction between tradition and originality. Consequently the Modern Movement itself was not entirely original nor free from the taint of historicism; nor was the nineteenth century entirely unoriginal in architecture. Nevertheless, Pevsner is justified in seeing in Late Modern architecture a shift away from originality and loss of authenticity. Pevsner's definition of the new historicism is worth quoting

3, 25, 29

since it poses the question of the significance of historicism in Arata Isozaki's architecture. According to Pevsner the return to historicism meant the imitation of, or inspiration by, much more recent styles, styles which had never previously been revived. Pevsner comments that, all reviving of styles of the past is a sign of weakness, because in revivals independent thinking and feeling matters less than the choice of patterns.[6]

Fundamental changes in style can occur by the replacement or supplementation of the existing form stock or failing this by the manipulation in new and original combinations, or the debasement of the same standard forms. There is a common basis of forms between Modern and Late Modern architecture much as happens in the Renaissance, Mannerist, Baroque, Rococo and Neo-Classical phases of post-Medieval architecture,[7] in which stylistic development is one of continuity with the forms undergoing great changes under the influence of new stylistic forces. The failure of technological development after the Second World War to drastically modify the form stock of the Modern Movement allowed internal artistic causes to assume a new importance in bringing about the transformation of the Modern style.

Admittedly historicism is a significant factor in Isozaki's architecture, and indeed his style is extremely individual and arbitrary, yet in the final assessment Isozaki cannot be dismissed simply as a historicist of the nineteenth century kind, or labelled a radical eclectic, as Jencks is wont to do. For one thing, he is far too original and creative in the way he uses his borrowed images, and for another, it is equally clear that he is a Mannerist. There can be little doubt about this since Isozaki's designs, far from being historicist in character, transform the architectural matter – his designs are never merely imitative.

Isozaki combines a profound understanding of the post-war crisis with a well considered plan for creating a new architecture from the debris of the Modern Movement. Modern architecture was extended but it could not be enhanced. It spread over more and more territory and was brought to bear upon more and individual problems. This situation contributed to the form fatigue and the pursuit of novelty in the 1950s. Isozaki responded to this situation by creating a highly idiosyncratic style; to a considerable extent Functionalism gave way to the cultivation of style as an end in itself. His individual style is articulate, intricate and sophisticated; Isozaki speaks in a silver-tongued language of great beauty and caprice.

The Tutelage of Kenzo Tange

Post-war Japanese architecture was dominated by Kenzo Tange whose preeminence is explained by his mastery of form and his extraordinary versatility. Tange is not only a great architect, he is also a gifted organiser and educator with a flare for focussing the creative talents of others. His dignified creative stance, unerring grasp of each situation as it arose, imbued the most uncompromisingly modern structural and construction techniques and planning with a subtle, pervasive Japanese expression, and won for him a virtual sovereign authority as the leading architect of his generation. Tange

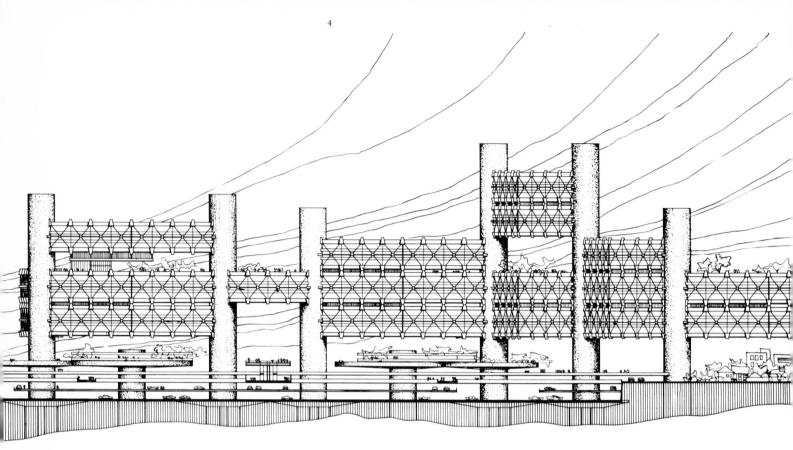

4 **Joint core project, 1962**
Tange's Yamanashi Press and Radio Centre
employed the same cylindrical core elements
and bridge spans

5 **Kenzo Tange: the Yamanashi Press
and Radio Centre, Kofu, 1967**

was the Japanese equivalent of Walter Gropius, indeed The Urbanists and Architects' Team (URTEC) was fashioned after Gropius's 'The Architects' Collaborative', TAC. It is a measure of his stature that Tange was able to assert that beautiful things are functional precisely because they are beautiful.

The lineage of Modern Japanese architecture, if it can be so described, is surprisingly simple. Arata Isozaki's architectural lineage commences with Tange, and through Tange extends to include Kunio Maekawa, a student of both Antonin Raymond and Le Corbusier – the two seminal influences on Modern Japanese architecture. Many of the best Japanese talents, among them Sachio Otani, Fumihiko Maki and Kisho Kurokawa, were students at one time in Tange's seminar. Isozaki joined Tange's seminar in 1952, and on his graduation from the University of Tokyo he entered Tange's office, remaining with him until 1963, when he left to establish his own practice. Isozaki's ten year apprenticeship spanned the most creative phase in Tange's career, from the Tokyo City Hall competition to the Yoyogi National Gymnasia.

Tange influenced Isozaki not least by his mastery of form, and was himself in turn influenced by Isozaki, who in addition to being an excellent draughtsman was also a fertile source of ideas. Isozaki's 'joint core' project for example, inspired such Tange projects as 3-D city planning, the Tsukuji Reurbanization Plan, the Yamanashi Press and Radio Centre, Kofu, and the Shizuoka Building in the Ginza. Isozaki contributed to the formulation of *A Plan for Tokyo* in 1960, and on leaving URTEC, collaborated with Tange on *28* the Plan for Skopje and the site planning for Expo '70. He also contributed the *40, 41* fundamental concept for the Festival Plaza at Expo '70. Isozaki and Tange are *47* very different personalities; Isozaki is an independent individualist, in contrast to the more traditionalist, co-operative Tange. As was customary, it was necessary for Isozaki to establish a separate architectural identity to Tange and to find a different way, which expressed his own ideas, of approaching architecture. This could prove painful when, in his 1962 essay, 'City Demolition Industry, Inc.' Isozaki launched a thinly veiled attack on the monolithic Tokyo Plan, in which the urban designer is represented as a professional hit man.

The break with Tange in 1963 was an important step in achieving artistic autonomy. Thereafter Isozaki cultivated a design orientation which was quite distinct from Tange's, and can be seen as a quite deliberate attempt on Isozaki's part to establish himself as an independent architectural personality. Two debts, the emphasis on method and the mastery of form, have survived in Isozaki's work. Moreover, Tange displays a consummate mastery of form, a capacity Isozaki also shares to an extraordinary degree. Isozaki is a syncretic stylist; for him style is independent of the programme and is something he imposes on the individual problem. In Tange's buildings style varies from and is organically linked to the programme thus Tange's is a classical aesthetic in which the opposing forces are held in balance. For Tange the goal is the establishment of a new urbanism, which serves as a focus for order in the surrounding chaos. Tange's buildings are immensely strong figures standing above a fragmented and confused Japanese urban cityscape. His buildings contain suggestions for binding the cities from the centre and spreading

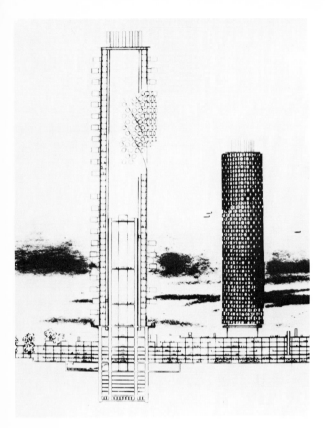

6 **Kiyonori Kikutake: Tower City, 1958. Section.**
Kikutake introduced the cylindrical core in his early Metabolism proposals

outwards. Isozaki's buildings can be seen as isolated fragments whose continuity depends on the completion of larger wholes, whose forms are based on the reiteration of a highly individual, and at times, arbitrary aesthetic.

Metabolism

Although Isozaki belongs to the same generation as the Metabolists Noboru Kawazoe, Kiyonori Kikutake, Fumihiko Maki, Masato Otaka and Kisho Kurokawa, he never at any time formally joined the Group. In an interview in 1971 with James Stirling Isozaki conceded,

'some of our tendencies are the same, but I always felt differently. I never became a member of the Metabolism Group.'[8]

Whilst Isozaki's aims differed from those of the Metabolism Group it is equally clear that he was strongly influenced by the Group's conception of form, particularly Kiyonori Kikutake's schemes. Isozaki's early buildings, notably the early megaskeletal series, are not genuine megastructures; what interested Isozaki was the adaptation of Metabolism's mega-aesthetic to the scale of the individual building, enlarging members – Tange also experimented with giantism – while giving the assembly of the beam and column elements, into which the frame has been simplified, a Constructivist expression.

The origin of the tubular hall of the Medical Hall, Oita, 1959–60, and the hollow hypertrophic beams of the Oita Prefectural Library, is consonant with the appearance of similar cylindrical tower structures in the early Metabolism projects of Kiyonori Kikutake. Kikutake's schemes were conceived prior to the formation of the Metabolism Group, and to an extent they supplied a focus for the establishment of the Group. Cylindrical service shafts feature in Kikutake's 1959, 'Tower City', and 1962 'Ocean City' proposals. Isozaki changed the function of the cylindrical shafts from that of support and service cores to a mere expressive one. Kikutake, for his part, had reversed the hierarchical relationship of the service towers and laboratory spaces in Kahn's Richard Laboratories by making the service towers permanent structural cores to which the transient habitable capsules could be attached. Consequently, although Isozaki was not himself a member of the Metabolism Group, Metabolism as the leading *avant-garde* movement in Japanese architecture in the 1960s deeply affected his development of architectural form.[9]

Isozaki was drawn into the Metabolism debate through his work for Tange on the 1960 *A Plan for Tokyo*, and in later proposals such as 'The Incubation Process', 1962, and 'City in the Air', 1962, out of which something quite different emerged, both in form and intention, to the schemes of the Metabolism Group. Even where, as in the 'City of the Air IV' scheme, the traditional column bracket arrangement is replaced by capsules inserted in a permanent cantilevered bracket support, Isozaki is chiefly interested in defining structuralist principles, and is only marginally interested in the technical aspects of his structure. In marked contrast to the biomorphic and mechanical motifs favoured by the Metabolists, Isozaki reverted to historical archetypes which are overwhelmed by an atmosphere of decay and disintegration. Fumihiko Maki's influence can be noticed in Isozaki's advocacy of Group Form and Plaza for the Skopje Plan. The idea of an instantaneous electric environment complete with robots for the Expo '70 Festival Plaza goes beyond anything envisaged by the Metabolists and appears to derive from the science fiction fantasies of Cedric Price and Archigram, especially the Monaco multi-entertainment centre.

For as much as Kisho Kurokawa's Takara Beautillon and capsule house in the Expo '70 theme pavilion, and Kiyonori Kikutake's Expo '70 tower represent the fulfilment of Metabolism's aims, so the 1975 Okinawa Ocean Expo, an event ideally suited to the aims of Metabolism, signalled its decline. In reality, with the exception of Metabolism stalwarts such as Kikutake, Metabolism as a movement began to lose ground even before the 1970 Exposition at Osaka, when its repetitive mechanical proposals were seen increasingly as anti-human and imposing a degree of conformity unacceptable even to the Japanese.

Isozaki and the Metabolism Group have little in common, for where the Metabolists viewed urban change as essentially a matter of technological adjustment, though this was given a thoroughly Japanese interpretation by means of analogies with growth in nature and cell replication, Isozaki was largely uninterested in change or in technology for its own sake except where technology served to reinforce his aesthetic interests. In the main Isozaki's career coincides with the decline of Functionalism as the leading dogma of the Modern Movement and its replacement by the new aesthetics of Mannerism. His aestheticism and interest in Western architecture reflect the increasing Westernisation of Japan in the 1960s and 1970s and may be seen as an attempt to assimilate the renewed invasion of Western culture.

Isozaki and His Contemporaries

The three outstanding personalities in Japanese architecture today are Fumihiko Maki (born 1928), Arata Isozaki (born 1931) and Kisho N. Kurokawa (born 1934). For over twenty years Kenzo Tange dominated Japanese architecture, but by the mid-1970s a serious illness, and the declining vitality of his architecture raised the question of who would replace him. In the October 1977 'Post-Metabolism' issue of *The Japan Architect*, Shozo Baba, its editor, assessed the claims of the leading aspirants to Tange's leadership and surveyed the younger generation or 'New Wave' of Japanese architects whose independence and diversity resisted any simple grouping which might have pointed to the future direction of Japanese architecture.

The two arch-rivals, Isozaki and Kurokawa, are quite different personalities; Kurokawa is the Napoleon of Japanese architecture, Isozaki its Che Guevara. Of the two, it is Isozaki who is the more gifted artist. Kurokawa, not to be underestimated as a designer, is a superb politician and prolific theoretician. Both Isozaki, as previously noted, and Kurokawa studied under Tange, so both are, in a sense, legitimate aspirants to succession. It is doubtful whether Isozaki takes the leadership contest all that

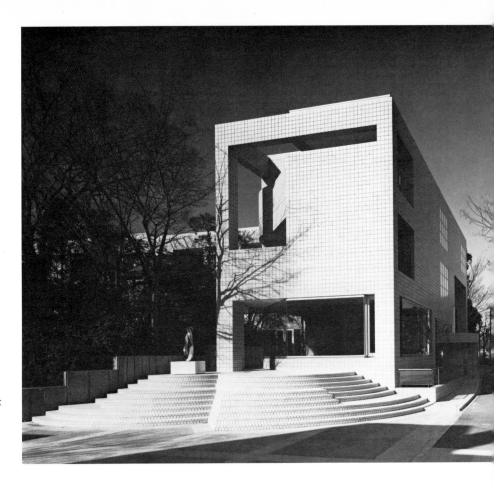

7 Fumihiko Maki: Hillside Apartment Complex, Tokyo, 1978
A conscious affinity arose between the architecture of Isozaki and Maki in the 1970s

seriously since his counter-culture attitude leaves little room for such architectural politics. Isozaki was the prime mover in the *New Wave of Japanese Architecture* exhibition and tour sponsored by the New York Institute for Architecture and Urban Studies late in 1978. The exhibition included work by Tadao Ando, Osamu Ishiyama, Monta Mozuna, Kijo Rokkaku, Kazuhiro Ishii, Hiromi Fujii, Toyoo Ito, Itsuko Hasegawa and Team Zo.

An original member of the Metabolism Group, Fumihiko Maki maintained a sceptical attitude to industrial urbanism, consequently, he did not find it necessary to repudiate Metabolism when it came under attack for its undue emphasis of technology. Not all Metabolist conceptions involved replaceable capsule houses and organic looking, if somewhat mechanical, megastructures. In 1968 Maki, Kikutake, and Kurokawa won the United Nations' Low Cost Housing, Lima Peru, competition with an entry which is remarkable for its modest construction and effective use of space.

Maki is a dispassionate man from a well-to-do family whose personality is reflected in an architecture that is assured and moderate. His early buildings were in a post-Bauhaus International Modern style, but more recently an increasingly eclectic taste is discernible in his work. A dialogue has developed between the architecture of Maki and Isozaki; the sculptured ceiling in Isozaki's Kamioka Town Hall recalls one by Maki in his Toyota Guest House, while the Hillside Apartment Complex, Tokyo, 1978, pays tribute to the Gunma Museum. The consistent international Modernism of Maki's early work has given way to an eclecticism which conforms to the new Mannerist sensibility that is much closer in style to Isozaki.

Isozaki is the leading exponent in Japan of the 'Post-Modern' quasi-Mannerist aesthetic. Following a tentative experimental phase in the late 1960s the new Formalism was well established by the beginning of the 1970s in New York and Philadelphia, and with less sureness in Los Angeles. It only remained for Isozaki to be affected by American and European developments for his own highly individual manner to assert itself and so produce a Japanese interpretation of the new style.

Under the circumstances he displayed a remarkable sentience in arriving, more or less independently, at a new quasi-Mannerist style. Gunma Museum of Art and Richard Meier's Bronx Development Centre have a number of features in common. It is apparent from a recorded discussion between Meier and Isozaki, that these similarities are entirely coincidental.[10]

Isozaki belongs to the Modernist stream, which is to say his architecture is the outcome of a dialectical response to Modern architecture involving the inversion and debasement of its forms. Not all the formal elements of the new quasi-Mannerist aesthetic are apparent in the architecture of Isozaki, or the next generation for that matter. Rather, the new style appears only partially. Some of the characteristics of the new aesthetic involve a preoccupation with basic geometrical forms, a preference for geometrical modes of architectural composition, and in Isozaki's case, the use of a generic geometrical code. This is paralleled by the imposition of a memorable overall gestalt on the building, and even anagramism. Cubic frameworks and semi-circular vaults feature prominently in Isozaki's later Neo-Classical works.

The tectonic shell is expressed as a thin tightly drawn skin. The debasement *127, 128* of the entire skeleton and the reinterpretation of all the individual form elements as components of a continuous skin, stretched or hung round the spatial form results in the triumph of two dimensionality and a kind of cardboard architecture.[11] The structural skeleton is debased by the extension *113* of the skin over the structural members, partial concealment of supports, and interruption of members. This process is heightened by warping the skin according to convex, concave shapes, to further emphasise its non-structural ornamental character. Fusion of the tectonic shell is accomplished by the imposition of an orthogonal grid over the entire skin, obliterating distinctions *106, 109* between wall, floor, and ceiling surfaces, between openings and walls, and inside and outside. The architecture of Hiromi Fujii is an extreme instance of the application of grids to the tectonic shell, both inside and outside. Ornament in various guises, whether as super graphics in Minoru Takeyama's case of gridded surfaces – a *horror vacuii* or *amor vacuii* – has become much more important and is used for its own sake, or is justified as an 'architectural sign'.

The Viennese *avant-garde* for a long time held a considerable fascination for Japanese architects, thus in 1920 the Bunri-ha-Kenchiku-hai Group was formed under the impact of Otto Wagner and the *Sezession*.[12] The Viennese

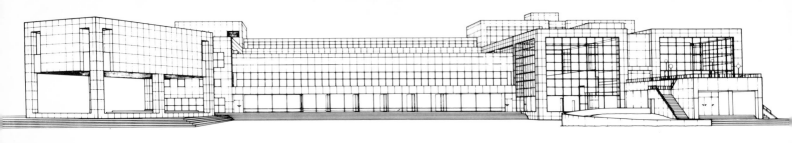

8 **Gunma Prefectural Museum of Fine
Art, 1974**
In both the Gunma Museum and the Bronx
Developmental Centre the skeletal frame is
obscured by a thin stretched skin of shiny
aluminium

9 **Richard Meier: Bronx
Developmental Centre, Bronx, 1970–77**

architects Adolf Loos and Hans Hollein are important influences on Isozaki.

An important difference between American and European quasi-Mannerist architecture and Japanese work, centres on the spatial quality of 'emptiness'. For Japanese architects spatial emptiness denotes the Buddhist paradox of substantial existence.[13] In Buddhist thought the basic meaning of existence is expressed in the truly non-existent. The metaphysically perfect spaces of

10 **Kazuo Shinohara: House in a Crooked Road, 1978**
Interior. Architectural emptiness is transformed by Shinohara with a positive statement of human existence.

Kazuo Shinohara inspired a generation of young Japanese architects, among them Toyoo Ito, with the concept 'emptiness'. The Japanese and Western interpretations of 'emptiness' are fundamentally different. In the West 'emptiness' conveys such negative associations as inner conflict, torment, and spiritual disintegration, whereas, for the Japanese 'emptiness' denotes the very essence of existence.

Quasi-Mannerist buildings – Kamioka Town Hall is a good example – are totally isolated from their environment. The impression conveyed by such buildings is of passivity and dependence; instead of constituting an ideal integrated and harmonious whole, quasi-Mannerist architecture emphasises inconsistency and ambiguity and a multiplicity of values.

Among the next generation, the architects closest to Isozaki are Kazuhiro Ishii, Takefumi Aida, Toyoo Ito, Hiromi Fujii and Monta Monzuna. Both Ishii and Aida construct their forms from cubes. Aida in addition imposes a single overall gestalt. The conceptualist architecture of Toyoo Ito is possibly closer in spirit to Isozaki than the others, his recent PMT building, Nagoya, 1978, recalls two works by Isozaki, the Gunma Museum and the Kamioka Town Hall.

An admirer of Aldo Rossi, Fujii is a Rationalist architect who once worked with Mangiarotti in Milan. His buildings are extreme and uncompromising illustrations of Rationalist ideas which he projects by inscribing grids on all their surfaces. His buildings exhibit overly complex and tortured geometries, additive cubic form, and submarine-like layered interiors. Isozaki rejects Rationalist ideology preferring Superstudio to Rossi, nevertheless, similarities of style, in the buildings of Fujii and Isozaki beg explanation. In this instance, it seems Isozaki may have been influenced by Fujii. The stained glass mandala window in the Kitakyushu Municipal Central Library display room represents an unexpected excursion into mystical symbolism found in the esoteric and geometrical designs of Mozuna. Mozuna's designs are saturated with the symbolism of esoteric Buddhism which he combines with a strong feeling for the magical significance of geometry. Thus geometry is a common factor linking Isozaki and Mozuna.

Stylistic Transformation

The Modern Movement was a stylistic revolution of equal, if not greater significance than Gothic or Renaissance. One of the challenges faced by architects in the second half of the twentieth century stems from the recognition that architecture has entered a phase of stylistic transformation similar in character to the changes in style which succeeded the Renaissance.
Isozaki has noted that,

'Modern architecture evolved a pattern whereby industrialisation penetrates the entire field. In itself, this is not unlike the Renaissance belief that classical order must be established in architectural space.
. . . in other words, the theory produced by Modern architecture has something of the nature of classicism. Today the myth of classical continuity has collapsed.'[14]

In post-Renaissance design the basic stock of forms and typical spatial structures were preserved, and although new ways of using them were found, they remained for all that substantially the same. No complete system of alien artistic forms was imposed replacing those derived from antiquity. Thus the architecture, from the Renaissance to Neo-Classicism, derived from a single source. The revolutionary character of the Modern Movement accustomed architects to view stylistic change as exclusively a matter of innovation at the level of the basic form stock, with the result that much energy has been directed at enlarging the form vocabulary. By and large, this activity has resulted in more of the same. In essence, Late Modern architecture recognises that stylistic change, for the moment, is mostly a matter of manipulating existing forms, even though the stock of forms has been enlarged by drawing on history.

Much as Mannerism in sixteenth century Italy represents the renunciation, debasement, and inversion of the classical procedures of the High Renaissance, so Late Modern architecture is sustained by the feeling that all the problems of the Modern Movement have been solved, and since these solutions were one-sided, they necessarily imply a renunciation of Modern architecture. The irony is that the extreme formalism of the new aesthetics is one-sided and so must succumb eventually. Where once Modern architecture emphasised spatial continuity, completeness of form, integration of technology and expression, identity of inside and outside, and suppression of applied decoration, Late Modern architecture now rejects such classical principles and insists on heterogeneous space, fragmented and incomplete form, discontinuity and discordance of parts, and rehabilitates decoration. Indeed, one of the very real dangers of the present situation is that architecture will become a kind of open-air decorative art. It is significant that the historical sources selected by Arata Isozaki for use in his architecture are drawn from periods of stylistic transition. In such periods of stylistic transformation, Isozaki observed, architecture is punctuated by

'. . . instances of this paradigmatic transfer, i.e. the manipulation of Renaissance architecture by Mannerists of the sixteenth century, the syntagmatic inversions of the Neo-Classicists in the eighteenth century, the decorative preoccupations of the nineteenth century eclectics, and finally the formal manipulation of the contemporary eclectics'.[15]

Isozaki's choice of the cube and semi-cylindrical vault as the *prima-materia* of his architecture after 1971 does not necessarily establish that a relationship exists between his work and Italian Renaissance architecture even when, as has been shown, the use of neo-Platonic solids is a feature of Renaissance design theory as set down by Alberti. The cube and barrel vault are composed in a pervasively unclassical fashion which, when taken with Isozaki's preference for architectural motifs and images drawn from sixteenth century Mannerism, provides further evidence of his anti-classical outlook. Isozaki often expresses himself by means of binary contrasts; cubic additive form and semi-cylindrical, or barrel vaulted form is just such a binary contrast. Cubic additive form corresponds to traditional Japanese architecture, while barrel vaulted form signifies Neo-Classical Western architecture. Both form types spring from his earlier megaskeletal trabeated form type, the cube being derived from the square beam and the semi-cylinder from the cylindrical core or pillar.

Individual Expression

'. . . at least, the minimum *sine qua non* for the kind of architect I have in mind is the presence of an idea unique to his inner self – that very idea which organically responds to the entire spectrum of phenomena including logic, design, reality and nonreality, but which, in the final analysis, is not even remotely related to them'.[16]

Arata Isozaki

Architecture, Isozaki insists, must begin with the individual. For him individualism is the ultimate source of architecture, whereas for Tange, and an earlier generation of Japanese architects, it had been society. The Renaissance discovery of the individual underlines Isozaki's emphasis of individual expression and his demand that architecture should articulate an idea unique to the architect. He echoes Descartes's proposition that the mind knows itself more immediately and directly than it can know anything else. Architecture, and here Isozaki means 'conceptual architecture', is subjective and must therefore begin with the consciousness of the individual. The primacy of self-consciousness in Isozaki's statements about architecture is symptomatic of the deep cultural transformation and Westernization of Japanese society which took place after the Second World War, and involved among other things a growing sense on the part of many young Japanese, of their separate individual identity.

Crisis

The crisis of Modern architecture was experienced as a personal crisis by architects who were unable to enhance or take architecture any further. Isozaki was not alone in feeling that all problems had been solved. What is remarkable in his case, is the acute personal quality of the experience and the Mannerist tone and imagery he afterwards invoked to describe his state of mind at the time. It has been said that Kurokawa's career swerves between extremes, and that Isozaki maintains a consistent course for extended periods, but is given to abrupt changes of direction. Such a break occurred in 1970 following his work on Expo '70 which left him exhausted. Six years later Isozaki wrote:

'Some years ago I announced my feeling that I could no longer produce anything. I did this because I caught a glimpse of the void; yet I had not yet discovered a method and shrank from what I saw. Suddenly I believed in the autonomous motivating power of form.'[17]

Vivid images are called on in a second, separate account:

'Once, when I was exhausted, dizzy, and at death's door, I unexpectedly saw an image of ruins. The vector on which I had been moving towards the future suddenly turned to the past. I experienced what might be called back lighting, and the sudden turn in direction suddenly threw the present into sharp focus.'[18]

The Mannerist quality of the last description with its references to 'ruins', 'back lighting', and 'sharp focus' recalls the strained atmosphere of Tintoretto's *Finding of the Body of St Mark*. The fascination with ruins is revealing since a ruin is a fragment that opens to the universe because it is incomplete. Much of Isozaki's architecture is incomplete and a fragment implying by its very incompleteness a larger whole.

Paul Frankl, writing about the impact of the classical stage on architectural development in the Renaissance, noted a phenomenon – he described it as a turning away from the principles of the Renaissance – which it can be argued, applies equally to Modern architecture in the twentieth century. He had this to say,

'The classical stage so viewed is stagnant and is therefore no longer bearable, especially for *those* artists who are fully conversant with its artistic principles. All problems seem to them to have been solved, and their innermost need for complete application of their creative abilities remains uncultivated.'[19]

Isozaki's crisis was brought on by a feeling that all the problems of Modern architecture had been solved and that there was nothing left for him to do. As he explains,

'It is now hopeless to dream of creating a leading principle that can point to new directions; all that is left for us to do is to manipulate already existing multifarious and extremely accurately worked out visual vocabulary items. . . . Under these conditions, the only thing the architect can do is employ this already known vocabulary in such a way as to develop his own individual method.'[20]

Isozaki's architecture is much richer and more complex than this statement suggests, yet this in essence is what lies behind Isozaki's development of his method. Eclecticism and Mannerism are two of a number of avenues of escape from the stylistic impasse. Mannerism has the advantage that it involves an inversion of the earlier style, and, in consequence, assures a degree of continuity through its manipulation of the stylistic elements of the previous phase. Isozaki's architecture is a mixture of both eclecticism and Mannerism. It needs to be recognised, however, that eclecticism is identified with Mannerism. Late Modern architecture is usually justified in terms of the failure of Modern architecture, and while the title of Isozaki's first book is *The Dismantling of Architecture* his writings contain little by way of a comprehensive critique. The years after 1930 witnessed the universalisation of the pervasive patterns of Modern architecture. Thereafter,

'There began', [Isozaki writes], 'the work of dismantling and reconstituting these same patterns,'

a process he believes will continue. Isozaki characterises the architect in the 1970s as one who is engaged in

'the work of manipulating the visual language left by past heroes to arrive at one's own conceptual world, or, equally possibly, to utterly disregard the possibility of a realisability of concepts'.[21]

Isozaki is much less concerned with carrying out a post-mortem than he is with finding a viable strategy for the present. His writings are characterised by a deep pessimism, induced perhaps by his feeling that all the previous common themes have vanished and the architect must, perforce, find his own personal ones:

'What this phenomenon fundamentally means is that any semblance of a common theme has vanished. Simultaneously, the process by which we come to know the world and the cosmos has become obscured. We have lost our sense of the connections between things, and we have become unable to generalise from events.'[22]

This, then, is the source of the architect's alienation, since the loss of common themes means that the architect is no longer able to relate his work to society. Heterogeneous space replaces homogeneous space, balance is suppressed and form fragmented, inconsistency and discordant relations prevail where once there was harmony.

2
Mannerism

Mannerism as the Key to the Architecture of Isozaki

What interests me about the architecture of Arata Isozaki is its affinity with Mannerism. The historical interpretation I wish to offer is of Arata Isozaki's architecture as a species of Mannerism, for it is Mannerism which in my view offers the key to interpreting his architecture. Such a selective viewpoint is justified only if it can be shown that kindred relations exist between Arata Isozaki's designs and Mannerism; that there is a family likeness. I am mindful of the dangers of historicism present in such an approach, since Isozaki's Mannerism, that is, the typological similarity presented by his mature post 1970 style, raises awkward questions regarding the periodic recurrence of styles. It needs to be emphasised therefore, that what is offered is not a theory in the form of a testable hypothesis, but merely an interpretation.

The late Dr Arnold Hauser's description of Mannerism in *Mannerism: The Crisis of the Renaissance and the Origin of Modern Art* (1965), serves, as few other instruments, to lay bare the aesthetic conventions, structure and meaning of Isozaki's architecture. Once Isozaki's architecture is recognised as a manifestation of Mannerist aesthetics, then much that appears irrational, formalistic, and bizarre falls into place.

Arata Isozaki is not alone in expressing Mannerist tendencies, since a Mannerist predisposition is latent in the early work of Le Corbusier. Indeed, the two leading trends in the 1970s, namely Mannerism and Neo-Classicism, were anticipated by Le Corbusier and Mies van der Rohe.

Robert Venturi belongs to the first generation of American mannerists. Moreover, *Complexity and Contradiction in Architecture* (1966) provides the earliest and clearest contemporary statement that we have of the new Mannerist attitude. The Venturi and Hauser books were published within a year of each other; Venturi wrote his, he tells us, in 1962, while Hauser's great work on Italian Mannerism was written in the early 1960s overlapping Venturi. Taken together they complement each other; Hauser traces the origins of Modern Art to the crisis of the Renaissance in the sixteenth century, whilst Venturi for his part, deploys much the same historical material to attack the classical standards implicit in Modern architecture in order to justify a point of view which, on closer examination, amounts to a new Mannerist sensibility.

The first generation of quasi-Mannerists was inspired by Louis Kahn in the United States, whose ideas derived in some measure from the French academic tradition inspired by Julien Gaudet. Venturi, Moore, Turnbull and Lyndon belong to this academic wing of American Mannerism which was succeeded somewhat later by a neo-Corbusian wing, made up by Richard Meier, Charles Gwathmey, Michael Graves and John Hejduk. The new phenomenon of American Mannerism quickly spread beyond the United States to Japan. Meanwhile, more or less independent, though not unrelated forms, appeared in such European centres as Vienna, London, and Florence.

A predisposition to Mannerism is discernible in Isozaki's early work, especially his sketches, in which the disturbance of scale and hypertrophy of architectural elements portends his later full blown Mannerism. Isozaki's incipient Mannerism was encouraged and nourished by developments in the United States, especially on the east coast. His architecture ought to be seen therefore, not as an isolated, distorted development within Japanese culture, but rather, as an extraordinarily accomplished display which was sustained and in part inspired by the much wider international Mannerist trend.

Isozaki was more fortunate than many of his American contemporaries, for instead of designing houses for the very rich, he was kept busy with a wide variety of public and commercial commissions, ranging in scale from small branch banks, to quite large prefectural art galleries. This varied clientele ensured that his buildings were well constructed with quality finishes prevailing in the public commissions, unlike the cheap timber or stucco construction of the Americans. Moreover, Isozaki's clients showed themselves to be remarkably tolerant in allowing a degree of freedom and experimentation which is rare outside Japan. These unusually favourable circumstances enabled him to create a quite remarkable series of buildings rivalling Palladio and Ledoux by their systematic elaboration of formal motifs.

Isozaki, like Palladio, built most of his works in provincial centres, and even though Oita cannot compare with Vicenza, it nevertheless stands in much the same relation to Tokyo, as did Vicenza to Rome in Palladio's day. Isozaki, unlike Palladio, chose to live in the great metropolitan centre of his day. In the instance of Isozaki, one is impressed by the obvious contrast between an immensely sophisticated architecture which is essentially international in character, and the unremarkable, downright provincial character of its setting.

Freedom and Constraint

In less than half a century the relationship of form and content in architecture has been reversed; initially, Early Modern architecture was sustained by the doctrine of Functionalism, which subordinated form. Formalism has once more returned to architecture. The new ascendency of form manifests itself in two contrasting stylistic tendencies. First, the revival of a 'universal'

11 **Parmigianino:** *Madonna del collo lungo,* **Florence, Uffizi**
Parmigianino's masterpiece includes such Mannerist traits as the exaggerated elongation of forms, irrational combination of subjects, disparate proportions and a most unintegrated representation of space

21

Mannerist aesthetic which was anticipated in the Dada and Surrealist movements of the 1920s, and second, the reassertion of Neo-Classical trends in late twentieth century architecture which derive immediately from the Modern Movement in the 1920s, and are often indissolubly entangled with others which proclaim the advent of a new kind of Mannerism, on one hand, and of a renewed Neo-Classicism, on the other. Both quasi-Mannerism and Neo-Classicism are rooted in Modern architecture, and so can be seen as an extension of ideas dormant in it. At the same time, their current prominence has been reinforced by the vehemence of the anti-Modern reaction which has encouraged the expression of stylistic tendencies which, until now, were latent in Modernism. The resuscitation in Late Modern of tendencies derived from the earlier phase of Modernism was stimulated by the crisis of the Modern Movement after the Second World War; Mannerism as an expression of the conflict between the spiritual and materialistic impulses of the time; and the Neo-Classicism as the resolution of the conflict on the basis of order and discipline.

Underlying the revival of Mannerism and Neo-Classicism is the immemorial dialectic between order and chaos, between freedom and constraint. Mannerism is identified with the search for freedom, the defiance of aesthetic codes, stimulating individualism, and a conception of reality as complex, contradictory, and essentially ambiguous. Neo-Classicism is the countervailing force to Mannerism in the 1970s; it stands for disciplined orderly form, austere expression and belief in technology. As such, it continues the alliance between expression and *techné* which was such a central feature of Early Modern architecture.

The most universal of all relations, Hegel held, was that of contrast or opposition. This led him to postulate the principle of 'dialectical movement' in every condition of thought or of things. Wolfflin adapted Hegel's principle to the discussion of style in art, and, although his thesis of stylistic periodicity, and an inner logic of style, of 'art history without names', has been largely discounted by later art historians as yet another instance of historicism,[1] the principle of 'dialectical movement' is useful in explaining developments in late twentieth century architecture.

The architecture of the 1970s stands in a more or less antithetical relation to Modern architecture, since it inverts many of the earlier conventions of Modernism. Furthermore, quasi-Mannerism is the outcome of a counter-Modern reaction, and Neo-Classicism is a regression to academic aesthetic values which initially contributed to Modernism, but were overlaid by such *avant-garde* movements as Futurism, Cubism, Elementarism, and Constructivism. Mannerism and Neo-Classicism are far from simple stylistic polarities to the extent that they may be present in the work of a single architect – sometimes they may occur in the same work. Where they do so, they are customarily used for contrast and to heighten the tension within the work. It would be a mistake, and an oversimplification of the present situation in architecture to see Mannerism and Neo-Classicism as antithetical styles having nothing in common with each other. Rather, they correspond to two conflicting impulses, the desire for order, and the desire for freedom. Neither Mannerism nor Neo-Classicism alone is able to wholly satisfy the expressive demands placed on them, consequently each includes features of the other.

In the architecture of Arata Isozaki Mannerist and Neo-Classical tendencies are inextricably linked; the Neo-Classical barrel vaults of the Fujimi Country Club and the Kitakyushu Memorial Library are bent in a quite arbitrary fashion that contradicts their underlying Neo-Classical expression. Isozaki gives order to his quasi-Mannerist designs by a strong cubic conceptual structure. Thus, in all his later works after 1970, total freedom and arbitrariness are never allowed to predominate, nor is order and pure geometry, at the other extreme, permitted to drive out all opportunities for the expression of humour, eroticism, and the arbitrary. Arata Isozaki's architecture is outside Western architecture, yet it is so closely dependent on it, as to provide a supremely revealing index to the complex movements affecting *avant-garde* Western architecture.

Isozaki's architecture moves between the two extremes of order and freedom which simultaneously attract, and can never, at the same time, be sustained for long; there is ever a desire to attain one or the other condition, however, neither goal is ever fully realised. In one series of works – his quasi-Mannerist architecture – the desire for freedom and expression of individual values and liberation from Modern architecture predominates; in the other, his Neo-Classical style, the desire for order and constraint takes charge, yet in neither is freedom or order permitted complete control of the architecture. Because Isozaki continually seeks to escape from the discipline of Japanese society the importance of individuality and freedom acquires an exaggerated importance; what is surprising, considering his cultural situation, is that so much discipline and formal order does manage to survive.

The essence of Mannerism is to be found in the tension between, and the union of, irreconcilable opposites. In his analysis of post-Medieval architecture Paul Frankl identified the highest collective polarity as the idea of constraint of personality which he saw as opposed by the idea of freedom of personality.[2] It is this union of irreconcilable opposites, with the two ideas confronting each other in the same work which constitutes the core of Mannerism. In the architecture of Isozaki the ideas of freedom of personality and constraint of personality are represented by Mannerism and Neo-Classicism, the two formal principles are frequently combined in the same work and made to confront each other; within Isozaki's world, the West stands for freedom and Japan is identified with constraint.

A feature of Isozaki's architecture is that for all the conscious striving for freedom and a chaotic arbitrary form, the underlying conceptual structure of his Mannerist compositions is fundamentally orderly. Isozaki is unable, in the final assessment, to escape the constraints of tradition. Paradoxically, his flight from Modern conventions merely takes him back to earlier historical prototypes.

The new quasi-Mannerism and Neo-Classicism are closely identified with Le Corbusier and Mies van der Rohe respectively. Traces of Palladian thought are evident in Le Corbusier, while the Neo-Classical order of Karl Schinkel is never far from Mies van der Rohe's mind.[3] Arata Isozaki's architecture is pervasively Mannerist both in his sensibility, and his forms, though there is a substantial Neo-Classical component, and in recent years, there has been a noticeable shift towards a strengthened Neo-Classical form under the influence of James Stirling.

The New Mannerist Sensibility

What parallels there are between Late Modern architecture and Mannerism proceed from an analogous response to an earlier phase of high classical achievement. The phenomenon of quasi-Mannerism in late twentieth century architecture is more a product of the logic of stylistic development than it is a child of the historical situation. External circumstances favoured the emergence of a species of Mannerism in the late twentieth century, however, its advent cannot be explained solely by reference to the social or cultural environment. In spite of the close parallels, the two stylistic phenomena are not the same; what they have in common is a similar aesthetic sensibility and view of the world. It is appropriate, therefore, to describe architecture which manifests the new Mannerist sensibility as quasi-Mannerism since the term implies that whereas the architecture resembles or simulates true Mannerism it is not quite the same thing.[4] A further difficulty is the lack of agreement about the correct historical definition of Mannerism itself.

The definition of Mannerism advanced by Dr Hauser (1965),[5] has been followed in the main in interpreting the architecture of Arata Isozaki. In Hauser's view alienation is the key to Mannerism, and, unlike some other historians, notably John Shearman (1967),[6] who confined Mannerism to the sixteenth century in Italy, and is content to treat it as an adaptation of a literary conception of *maniera* involving an obsession with style for its own sake, emphasising such qualities as facility, effortless accomplishment and virtuosity. Hauser is at pains to explain the psychological mainsprings of Mannerism. Shearman avoids the obvious question which Hauser explores with great insight, namely, the relation of Mannerism to the social and cultural environment.

Mannerism makes a statement about the alienation of the individual from society, and a view of the world

'. . . based, not merely on the conflicting nature of occasional experience, but on the permanent ambiguity of all things, great and small, and on the impossibility of certainty about anything,'[7]

which it expresses by the linking of irreconcilable opposites in the same work, and the exploitation of paradox. Hauser insists that

'a proper understanding of Mannerism can be obtained only if it is regarded as a product of tension between classicism and anti-classicism, naturalism and formalism, rationalism and irrationalism, sensualism and spiritualism, traditionalism and innovation, conventionalism and revolt against conformism; for its essence lies in this tension, this union of apparently irreconcilable opposites'.[8]

The dialectic principle underlies the entire Mannerist outlook inasmuch as the discord in the work of art expresses the conflict of life itself and the ambivalence of all human experience; what the artist seems to be trying to demonstrate is that artistic values do not have to be, or actually should not be, simple.

Explanations of Mannerism vary as widely as its definition; John Shearman rejects any suggestion that it is associated with tension or collective neurosis and argues instead that it was,

'. . . on the contrary, the confident assertion of the artist's right, which he seemed to have regained in the High Renaissance, to make something that was first and last a work of art; . . .'.[9]

The controversy over the origin of Mannerism is not without importance since whichever interpretation is adopted affects our conception of Mannerism. For John Shearman Mannerism is an extravagantly accomplished style of excess which celebrates facility and is obsessed with style for its own sake. Arnold Hauser asks why Mannerism is obsessed with style, why it is essentially derivative and is inspired less by nature than by other works of art?

'What', [he asks], 'is the significance of the prevalence of metaphorism, paradox, artificiality, fragmentation of form, spatial incoherence and the combination of opposites or duality?'[10]

The key to Mannerism, according to Arnold Hauser, is alienation. He firmly maintains that it should not be seen as a passive symptom and product of alienation, that is,

'an art that has become soulless, extroverted and shallow'

but more correctly

'as an expression of unrest, anxiety and bewilderment generated by a process of alienation of the individual from society and the reification of the whole cultural process.'[11]

The confusion over the proper interpretation of Mannerism arises partly from its diverse character which lends itself to selective interpretations. Hauser and Shearman illustrate the two leading interpretations. Shearman advances a view of Mannerism as fundamentally one of style or *maniera*, Hauser explores the social and cultural dimensions of Mannerism and demonstrates that its anti-classical features are not exclusively a matter of stylistic development, and in doing so, is able to show that Mannerism coincides with the emergence of the Modern outlook. Such a view of life, August Heckscher contends, is an attainment of maturity, and Robert Venturi quotes Heckscher with approval:

'The movement from a view of life as essentially simple and orderly to a view of life as complex and ironic is what every individual passes through in becoming mature. But certain epochs encourage this development, in them the paradoxical or dramatic outlook colours the whole intellectual scene. . . Then equilibrium must be created out of opposites. Such inner peace as men gain must represent a tension among contradictions and uncertainties . . . a feeling for paradox allows seemingly dissimilar things to exist side by side, their very incongruity suggesting a kind of truth.'[12]

The value of Hauser's analysis of Mannerism lies in his demonstration that it is not simply anti-classical, accordingly,

'a proper understanding can be obtained only if it is regarded as the product of tension between classicism and anti-classicism. . . '.[13]

Robert Venturi's polemic, *Complexity and Contradiction in Architecture* advances a well considered argument against the prevailing classical standards of Modern architecture and so is as much an anti-classical as it is an anti-Modern statement.

Complexity and Contradiction in Architecture is the single most important post-war polemic on architecture. Its importance derives from its identification and denunciation of classical standards of Modern architecture and Venturi's extraordinarily prescient advocacy of Mannerism as an alternative to classicism. Hauser and Venturi both agree on the defects of classicism. Hauser writes that

'the classical revolt against Renaissance classicism was directed chiefly against the over-simplification it imposed on the variety of phenomena. In every Mannerist work the artist seems to be trying to demonstrate artistic values do not have to be, or actually cannot be, simple.'[14]

Venturi suggests that architects

'can no longer afford to be intimidated by the puritanical language of orthodox modern architecture,'

and then goes on to define what, on examination, amounts to a personal statement of Mannerist preferences.

'I like elements which are hybrid rather than "pure", compromising rather than "clean", distorted rather than "straightforward", ambiguous rather than "articulated", perverse as well as impersonal, . . .'[15] etc.

Lest there be any doubt that he is recommending a return to Mannerist values, Venturi states that

'the desire for a complex architecture with its attendant contradictions, is not only a reaction to the banality or prettiness of current architecture, it is an attitude common in the Mannerist periods: the sixteenth century in Italy or the Hellenistic period in classical art; and is also a continuous strain seen in such diverse architects as Michelangelo, Palladio, Borromini, Vanbrugh, Hawksmoor, Soane, Ledoux, Butterfield, some architects of the shingle style, Furness, Sullivan, Lutyens, and recently Le Corbusier, Aalto, Kahn and others.'[16]

The problem with quasi-Mannerism in late twentieth century architecture is that history is not supposed to repeat itself. To all intents quasi-Mannerist architecture is not identical with sixteenth century Italian Mannerism, in so far as the basic form stock of the two architectures is entirely different. There is, however, as a comparison of Venturi and Hauser reveals, a surprising identity of outlook on matters of form. Venturi misunderstands Mannerism, by insisting that it is in some way more fit and true to reality than the classical. Neither the classical nor Mannerism are dedicated to naturalism, each is highly selective in what it takes from experience. The classical work seeks out and emphasises that which is common and universal in human experience, the Mannerist selects and heightens that which is different. Hauser reminds us that

'the artists and writers of the Mannerist period were not only aware of the insoluble contradictions of life, they actually emphasised or intensified them.'[17]

He points out that because moments of classicism are in reality a tremendous *tour de force*,

'an achievement wrung from the age by force and not plucked like naturally grown fruit',[18]

classicism is unstable and short lived. Mannerism is one of several possible outcomes following the decay of the classical phase. Mannerism and classicism represent contrasting ways of looking at the world; one emphasises unity and that which is common and universal to all human experience. Mannerism by contrast, eschews the classical simplification of reality by replacing the organic unity of a work by duality, and seeking instead, through the dialectic, a collection of fragments which when taken together, convey a sense of the complex contradictory nature of reality. Far from being a straightforward, or even naive account of the real world, Mannerism insists on eliminating those very qualities which the classical takes and heightens. Both the classical and Mannerism treat the real world in ways which depart from reality, thus Mannerism

'is not so much a picture of reality as a collection of contributions to such a picture.'[19]

Each generation discovers the past anew; recognition of the 'retroactive power' of the present, as Nietzsche called it, is not necessarily the same thing as projecting on the past ideas and experiences which properly belong to the present. One of the criticisms of Hauser's interpretation of Mannerism is that he has projected twentieth century ideas of alienation, narcissism, inner tension, conflict and self awareness onto the sixteenth century. This is why, so the argument runs, it is possible to find such striking parallels between the art and architecture of the two periods. It is equally plausible to argue that the twentieth century has been sensitised by such developments as expressionism and surrealism, cinematography and psychoanalysis, to the sixteenth century whose artistic endeavours are in line with our own objectives.

Mannerism is considerably more than the expression of the tension between classicism and the anti-classical; it is typified by inorganic anti-classical aesthetics, a revolt against simplification and the principles of multiplicity, duality, fragmentation of form and space, tendency to spatial depth, and suppression of depth in architectural facades. Consciousness of 'style' is accompanied by artificiality and isolation from nature, formalisation of artistic expression and eclecticism. Consequently, Mannerism draws its inspiration from other styles. The derivative or eclectic nature of Mannerism does not lead to a direct imitation of earlier styles, hand in hand with distortion, *11* elongation or exaggeration of forms, there is an inversion of conventions. Mannerism makes extensive use of disguises of the spirit, and through such devices as distortion, projection, mirrors, masks and metaphors it expresses the individual's alienation from his 'self' and the world, and his retreat into secondary narcissism.[20] The metaphor reflects nothing so truly as the writer himself, hence, the exaggerated display of individualism and subjectivity, sensibility and arbitrariness of Mannerism. The use of paradox and the dream are favourite Mannerist devices. Mannerism is quintessential art in so far as meaning is derived from the spirit of the expressive medium itself. The Mannerist is inspired less by nature than by other works of art.

The Quest for Style

One way of explaining Mannerism is to see it as quintessential art, and the Mannerist as one who is inspired 'less by nature than by other works of art'. Mannerism is substantially derivative, drawing its inspiration from other styles and a deliberate reaching back to an earlier style. This accounts for the obvious eclecticism of Isozaki's architecture. Meaning arises from the spirit of the expressive medium itself, not so much filling it with content as deriving content from it. Mallarmé expressed a similar view in a remark addressed to Degas in which he stated

'that poems are written not with ideas, but with words'.[21]

Mannerism is essentially derivative, it necessarily

'. . . meets its formal requirements with the means of expression of its predecessors, develops a new formal language only to a limited extent, and seeks to compensate for this lack of originality by the partial exaggeration and distortion of traditional formal means'.[22]

Mannerism is essentially an art of deformation, by his distortion, inversion and decomposition of form the Mannerist seeks to differentiate his product from the source which inspired it. Hauser goes on to add

'that the whole outlook of the age revolves round the idea of distortion, concealing and obscuring reality and putting substitute forms in its place.'[23]

Because Mannerism is an artificial style inspired by other art, artistic expression is formalised and the artist relies increasingly on the use of formulae instead of observation of nature for the details of his compositions. The artificiality, formalism, and isolation of Mannerism from life is inherent in its origin, the Italian word *maniera* was borrowed from French courtly literature of the thirteenth to fifteenth centuries.[24] Mannerism takes its meaning from one particular usage, which translated, means *style*. Vasari adapted *maniera* from the literature of manners, where it was used to describe a desirable quality of deportment, so as to identify painting originating in a cultural, not natural experience. Whereas the painters of the fifteenth century and the early sixteenth century are described by Vasari as painting from nature – *di natura* – those of the late sixteenth century are said to paint by manner – *di maniera* – that is to say, they cultivated a Mannerism which they could repeat without having to refer back to nature.

Metaphorism is fundamental to both Isozaki's architecture and to Mannerism. Metaphor is the most important means of expression in Mannerist literature, and indeed, metaphor represents the quintessence of the poetic apprehension of reality. Arnold Hauser maintains that metaphorism is tied to narcissim to the extent that things are not so much compared as brought into relationship with the writer. Consequently, the metaphor reflects nothing so much as the author himself.[25] The mirror performs a similar role to metaphor and is a popular device in Mannerist painting. Mirrors and highly polished or reflective surfaces occur in the main stair of the Gunma Prefectural Museum of Modern Art, 1972, and the entrance of Shukosha building, 1975, to mention two examples. Their purpose is to undermine reality and increase the degree of illusion and a dreamlike quality. This accounts for Isozaki's preference for such metaphors as twilight, shadow, and darkness.

The two leading principles in Isozaki's work, metaphorism and conceptual fusion, apply pre-eminently to poetry. The role of 'conceptual fusion' in poetry is to break through the conceptual bonds with which language constrains us. Leech notes that

'if one of the major roles of language is to reduce experience to order, to "prepackage" it for us, then the poet is the person who unties the string. It is in this context that the "irrational" or "counterlogical" character of poetry becomes explicable.'[26]

53

52, 77

36

It is not surprising, therefore, to find that such counterlogical devices as metaphor and paradox are closely connected with both poetry and Mannerism. In the final assessment, Isozaki's method finds its closest parallels with poetry, and semantics, while it offers an intellectual model, turns out to be much less important. The notion of an architecture of pure form provides a further connection with poetry for

'Mannerist poetry is not only like any other, the art of words tied to words and rooted in the nature of language, but also arises out of the spirit of language, not so much filling it with content as deriving content from it.'[27]

One role of Isozaki's conceptual structures of abstract cubes is precisely that, for the content of the architecture is derived from the arrangement of cubes which are of necessity empty and transparent.

The emphasis on semantics is misleading, inasmuch as the means employed are nearest that of the poet, semantic theory merely provides an intellectual model and rationale on which to found his poetics. Semantics is itself a metaphor which when it is applied to architecture undermines objectivity. For theoretical purposes, such an equation of language and architecture is invalid. Isozaki's poesy is opposed, not only to the Rationalism of Modern architecture, which it frequently parodies, but also to the direct expression of feeling. Isozaki's method embraces two operations, the paradigmatic or selectional, and syntagmatic or combinational axes of language. The second principle, that of constituent structure refers to ways in which larger linguistic

12 **West Japan General Exhibition Centre, Kitakyushu, 1975–7**
Isozaki applied the metaphorical concept 'sea-roof' to the design of the suspended roof of the exhibition space

units are built up out of smaller elements. Conceptual reorganization occurs when, as in the use of metaphor, the poet combines two contrastive concepts in such a way as to dissolve their separateness. Isozaki also creates a new alignment of meaning by combining unconnected motifs in the same work. Leech gives the example of *mere hengst* ('sea-stead') from an Anglo-Saxon poem as a metaphor for ships;[28] a comparable example from Isozaki is the 'sea-roof' metaphor of the Kitakyushu Municipal Exhibition Hall, 1975–7, in which the roof over the hall is identified in its imagery with sunlight striking the surface of the sea. Thus, the metaphorical concept 'sea-roof' is applied to the roof of the exhibition hall. This poetic use of visual metaphor by Isozaki achieves a communicative effect which is 'beyond architecture'. Furthermore, Isozaki is able to take his revenge on the 'stereotyped ideas' of orthodox Modern architecture. This liberates architecture and counteracts the single-dimensional methodology of Modern architecture, which arises from its all too pervasive expression of industrialism and use of the 'machine' analogy.

Isozaki says of his procedure that it requires

'the manipulation of the universal language left by past heroes to arrive at one's own conceptual world, or equally, to utterly disregard the possibility or realizability of concepts.'

He adds that, furthermore,

'in this case the mode of manipulation and means of transformation of the specified "language" becomes a key to my work.'[29]

The method of juxtaposing and manipulating visual metaphors is not strictly the same as word ordering in language, that is syntax, and is only roughly similar. The syntagmatic parallel arising from his combination of metaphors did not escape Isozaki, as his remark on the opposition of Formalism and Functionalism indicates; Formalism, Isozaki proclaims,

'. . . interprets architecture as form and makes form independent. It adopts the position that it is possible to develop new meanings by means of the management of forms. Form gives birth to meaning. . .'.[30]

Recently Isozaki has emphasised the rhetorical mode of expression, and in doing so, Koji Taki, the Japanese critic, observed of Isozaki that,

'he has progressed in a dimension in which he gives configuration to a kind of relationships manipulation. At the bottom of these configurations (or spaces) is a series of semantic oppositions. . .'.[31]

Metaphor

Isozaki's architecture teems with images and associations so that none seems to predominate, yet in spite of this overloading of the architecture with metaphors, sometimes his buildings are a single metaphor. The whole architecture is, if you like, a vast metaphor, charged with a rich profusion of secondary metaphors. At times the work as a metaphor is dominant, as in the Nagasumi and Ropponmatsu branches of the Fukuoka Sogo Bank where there is hardly any place for detailed metaphors of any kind. In other works such as the home office of the Fukuoka Sogo Bank, Fukuoka, the profusion of metaphors overwhelms a weak primary metaphor.

By its exaggerated individualism, sensibility and arbitrariness, Isozaki's

106–8
109–10
90
126

excessive metaphorism shows signs of a struggle against the deadening of spontaneity and the mechanisation of reactions. As a Mannerist in Neo-Classical guise, Isozaki's buildings pretend to use forms which are classical in origin, which none the less, are threatened by a compulsive use of metaphorical imagery. This leads to the dissolution of a rational programme and its replacement by a free exchangeability of images, guided more by the affinities of the forms themselves than by use or intention. Developments such as these presage the negation of reason, function, and all external disciplines to which the architect ought to be prepared to submit.

Isozaki's metaphors are a means of evading reality – they disguise his flight from Functionalism. The metaphor becomes more real and substantial than the fabric of the building itself. They reflect nothing so truly as Isozaki himself, for things are not so much compared as brought into relationship with him.

The passion for metaphors and their profusion throughout Isozaki's architecture arises from a sense of life which views everything as being in a state of continuous change and interaction. The feeling of loss and uncertainty which underscores the metaphorism of Isozaki's architecture is identified in his statement,

'We have arrived at a point where we have no choice but to regard everyday space as something inexplicable in any but topological terms, where alien qualities mingle indiscriminantly, where time runs in all directions at once; where thus our focus is multilateral, where the dream of establishing a fixed point of view has vanished, and where this overlapping, other-dimensional space twists in kaleidoscopic patterns.'[32]

A metaphor may occur in isolation or reappear again and again. Whatever their frequency, however, a number of themes are common to all the metaphors, themes which, often as not, are closely identified with Mannerism. Examples of some of the more prevalent metaphors are the sacred pillar, mechanical tubes, Platonic solids, Palladio, void, darkness, shadow, twilight, ruins, letters, and the human face. There is a degree of confusion in Isozaki's writings[33] about the difference between quotation and metaphor. For example, many of the sources he lists as quotations, such as Marilyn Monroe, the Italian Palazzo, or Palladio, are not quoted, but appropriated and converted into an architectural motif whose connection with the original thing is usually slight. The silhouette of Marilyn Monroe's torso in the wall opening of the gatehouse of the Museum of Art, or the restaurant of the Kitakyushu Municipal Central Library is not so much a 'quotation' as an allusion to Marilyn Monroe. The clerestory roof over the main lecture hall of the New Building for the Oita Medical Hall is not a naturalistic representation of a strato cumulus cloud formation so much as a roof like a strato cumulus cloud, a simile in fact.

Duality is a leading principle and sometimes binary contrasts or visual opposition is brought into play. The ying yang concept illustrates the principle of dialectic movement and points to the importance of contrastiveness for metaphorism. The metaphors identify a number of important concerns in Isozaki's architecture: the sacred pillar, mechanical tube, Platonic solids and Palladio signify a classical leaning in Isozaki's style. Such metaphors as void, twilight and shadow express the sense of the unreality and

heightened illusionism; the apprehension of life as insubstantial and subject to decay, and of things as incomplete fragments, as elements of a larger ghostly whole is implied by the metaphor of ruins and the imagery of bodily decomposition in the Electric Labyrinth for the 14th Triennale, Milan, in 1968.

Eroticism is a pervasive factor and appears in a variety of guises, at first almost innocently in the naked outline of Marilyn Monroe, an ambiguous sexual imagery developed around the idea of hermaphrodite, while in such works as in A's Residence and the entrance way to the Gunma Prefectural Museum of Modern Art the imagery is explicitly phallic. Hauser observed that pornography, when it first appeared in the sixteenth century, was the sign of a bad conscience. The eroticism of Isozaki's metaphorical imagery displays none of this; for Isozaki the duality of male and female is paramount, and is made the vehicle for exploring other dualities such as Japan and the West, and cube and cylinder. The metaphor of hermaphrodite is important because it explores the ambiguity of the sexual polarity of male and female. Wherever Isozaki uses explicitly phallic forms these are opposed by a vaginal space, as in A's Residence and the Gunma Museum. The phallic entrance to the Museum is a parody of Ledoux's scheme for the Oikema or House of Passion. The Marilyn Monroe metaphor was inspired by Andy Warhol's series of silk screen prints in 1962 in which Monroe was deified as a modern goddess of love and the personification of female sexuality.

The Marilyn Monroe silhouette is a recurrent theme. It started as a pattern template in 1966 and was applied to plywood chairs, later an idealized silhouette of Marilyn Monroe's provocative torso was projected onto the gatehouse of the Gunma Museum, the outline of the restaurant of the Kitakyushu Library and the entrance foyer facade to Kamioka Town Hall. The persistence of the Marilyn Monroe metaphor is a measure of the fascination which big bosomed blonde females have for Japanese men. The sexual duality is reinterpreted as the duality of cube and tunnel vault; cubic additive form is conceived of as masculine and complete, whereas, serpentine tunnel vaults are regarded as feminine and incomplete.

The human face is a recurrent image in Isozaki's facades. Sometimes the

14

13 **Photo montage for the 14th Triennale, Milan, 1968**
The metaphor of ruins expresses a view of reality as fragmentary

14 **Marilyn Monroe nude profile**
Eroticism is a pervasive factor in Mannerism

15 **Marilyn Monroe chairs, Art Library Kitakyushu City Museum of Art, 1972–5**

16 **Restaurant, Central Library of the City of Kyushu**
The roof profile recalls the Marilyn Monroe silhouette

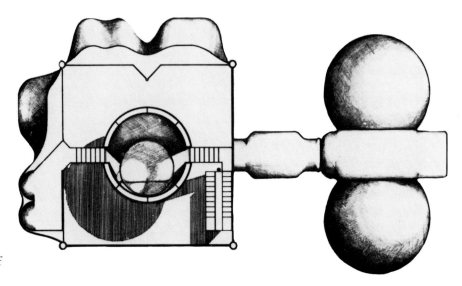

17 A's Residence, 1968–9
The explicitly phallic and vaginal form of
the project is a reminder of the erotic side of
Mannerism

**18 Giulio Romano: Palazzo del Té,
1524–34**
The dropped triglyphs on the court facade
is symptomatic of the Mannerist debasement
of the entire skeleton and reinterpretation of
all the individual corporeal forms as
components of a continuous skin

facial image is so abstract and fleeting as to be unrecognisable, nevertheless, its presence in the Fujimi Clubhouse, Ropponmatsu branch of the Fukuoka *48* Sogo Bank, Gunma Museum Exhibition Hall and facade of the Y Residence leave no doubt as to its importance.

The metaphor of 'ruins' is suggestive of a feeling of instability and the untrustworthiness of the material world. On the walls of the Hall of Giants of the Palazzo del Té brutish giants overbalance and fall amid the crashing stones. Lest the psychological import of the scene escape us, Giulio Romano dropped every third triglyph around the courtyard to reinforce the atmosphere of impending disaster and ruin. Two things are implied by the 'ruins' metaphor. Firstly, it is connected with a state of anxiety and uncertainty, and secondly, it symbolises the loss of wholeness, integration and balance. The 'ruin' is a nostalgic momento of an earlier time when forms were complete, self-sufficient, and whole. It is a fragment whose very incompleteness is a reminder of the complete form from which it has been taken by

19 **Shukosha Building, Fukuoka, 1974–5**
In much the same way as Giulio Romano's dropped triglyph the spalled travertine facing is used by Isozaki to express decay and disintegration

removing or omitting parts. Isozaki's method of 'slicing' is a procedure for turning fragments out of Platonic solids, 'projection' obscures the completeness of the Platonic solids and 'amplification' transfers their scale from that of the solid to that of the smallest unit composing the universal grid. The 'City in the Air', 1960–62, collage of the incubation process, is the earliest example; later in the Electric Labyrinth for the 14th Triennale Milan, 1968, a ruined megastructure is introduced into the devastated landscape of Hiroshima. The split travertine facing of the Shukosha building is used in much the same fashion as Giulio Romano's dropped triglyph to express the theme of decay and disintegration.

Spiritualisation of form is expressed in a variety of ways; forms may be deprived of their sensation of solidity and made to appear weightless. Isozaki's 'amplification' procedure is a means of increasing the abstraction and remoteness from nature or artificiality. The rigorous application of a universal Cartesian grid to all the surfaces, particularly the exterior, has the effect of increasing the abstraction of the forms and reducing their appearance of mass and solidity, the building no longer weighs down upon the ground and, instead, it appears to levitate and lack weight altogether.

The dematerialisation of form is reinforced by reducing visual contrast with soft colours in a 'twilight' like atmosphere, and by covering the outside of the building with a thin highly reflective mirror-like skin stretched tightly over the concealed inner form. The thinness of the surface membrane and its high reflectivity gives an impression of minimal weight and substance, and the thickness of the forms is perceived as no greater than the mirror itself. The denial of the skeleton and the accompanying formalisation of structure, are corollaries of the dematerialisation of form. Dematerialisation is one of the most significant innovations of Mannerism. The pair of square tubes of the Kitakyushu Municipal Art Museum do not bear down upon the substructure of the building so much as skim across the silhouette of the hill. The source for these forms is of course El Lissitsky's *Wolkenbügel* proposal for eight gateway towers at the intersections of Moscow's inner ring road. The illusion of hovering weightless forms occurs much earlier in Western art in such Mannerist works as Tintoretto's *St Mark rescuing a slave*.

Inner darkness is another device for negating substance; by establishing inner space within the architecture and adjusting the light intensity a quality of unreality is increased.[34] The reception lobby of the executive offices suite of the Fukuoka Sogo Bank Headquarters building contains just such a demonstration of the concept 'darkness'. The motif of an inner central spine of deep space was introduced in the Oita Prefectural Library, 1966 with the core space captured and held between a pair of double walls. Later examples of the same kind are the Fukuoka Sogo Bank Headquarters, the Kitakyushu Muncipal Art Museum and the Gunma Prefectural Museum of Modern Art. All these buildings possess an empty longitudinal spine bounded by two thick walls or double walls and with the buildings spread out perpendicular to the spine. The spines of the Oita branch of the Fukuoka Sogo Bank and the annex of the Oita Medical Hall avoid the expression of 'darkness'. Darkened space diminishes the spectator's awareness of the surrounding enclosure and focusses his awareness on his individual consciousness.

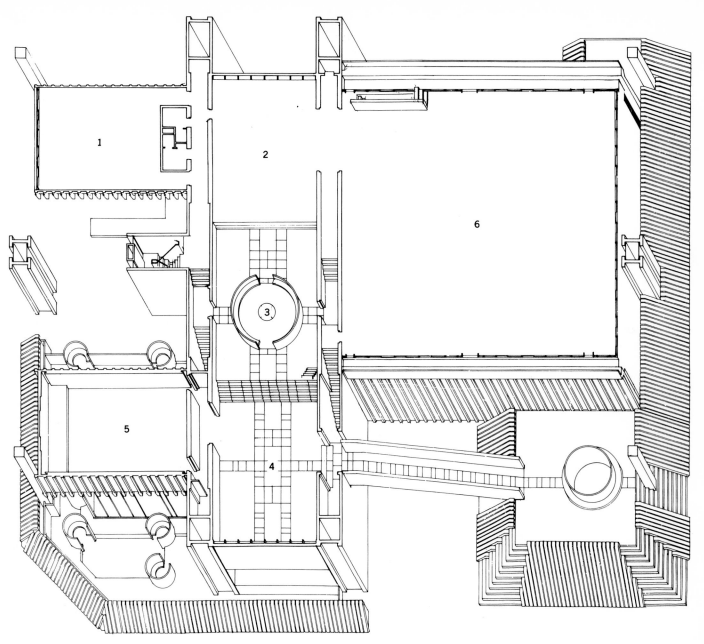

20 **Oita Prefectural Library, Oita, 1962–6**
Oblique projection. The entrance hall demonstrates the principle of an inner central spine contained by a pair of double walls and expressive of 'darkness'
Key: 1. service; 2. reference; 3. browsing; 4. entrance hall; 5. projection booth; 6. reading room

21 **Gunma Museum of Fine Art, Takasaki, 1971–4**
The irrational reverse perspective of the marble stepped platform is meant to awaken a feeling of uncertainty and alienation from reality

22 **Tokyo branch, Fukuoka Mutual Bank, 1970–71**
Letters have been used structurally to construct the street facade

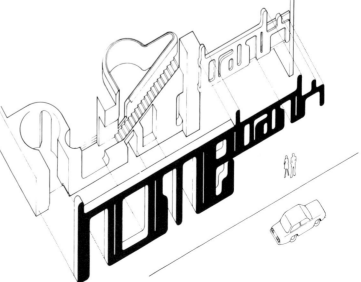

38

Illusion is a means of heightening the spectator's mistrust of his perceptions and of awakening the feeling that there is no firm ground anywhere beneath his feet – this increases the individual's alienation from reality. Two examples of deliberate illusion in Isozaki's architecture deserve mention. They are the reverse perspective large marble platform at the end of the entrance lobby of the Gunma Prefectural Museum of Modern Art, and the fake doors in the *58a* entrance lobby of the Shukosha building.

The Renaissance discovery of perspective was used as an aid to realism in painting, however, architects were quick to realise that perspective could be manipulated to control the perception of depth. Bramante introduced a false perspective in the sanctuary of S. Satiro, and an impressive perspective effect is produced in the Scala Regia by the convergence of the rising barrel vault. Palladio constructed a series of exaggerated perspectives in the permanent scenery of the Teatro Olimpico. In the entrance lobby of the Gunma Museum the marble platform converges towards spectators instead of vanishing in the distance, as is more usual, and this results in a sculptural paradox. Here the perspective effect is used in an irrational way that contradicts normal vision.

An anagram involves the transposition of the letters of a word or phrase to form a new word or phrase. Something like this occurs when the letters of a word are used to construct the facade of a building as happens in the Tokyo branch of the Fukuoka Sogo Bank, or when the vault form of the Fujimi Country Clubhouse is fashioned in the shape of a question mark. The *67* contradiction in scale enhances the quality of illusion, unreality and ambivalence. Meaning is dissociated from the letters and the form of the letters alone acquires a new importance. This phenomenon is but another instance of the Mannerist separation of form from content and advancement of form.

Wholeness and Fragmentation

Isozaki's architecture is at once a whole, and a collection of fragments, depending on how it is viewed. Such a contradiction of levels, the phenomenon of 'Both – And' in architecture, as Venturi preferred to call it, arises because Isozaki's interpretation of Mannerist form is ambivalent. At the surface level there is much diversity, opposition and contradiction; consequently his architecture becomes an assembly of heterogeneous parts. He then fuses the assembly in an orderly array of cubes or subordinates form to the tunnel vault. Both the cube structures and the serpentine tunnel vaults are incomplete, a quality which is enhanced in the former by breaking symmetry, or by failing to complete it. The tunnel vault is a fragment cut from a length of vault. In additive cubic form the constituent cubes are complete, it is only the total form built additively out of these cubic elements which lacks coherence and wholeness. The tunnel vault is, by its very nature, a fragment so although its form implies a homogeneous and consistent extension of space the tunnel vault, unless it assumes a ring shape, must inevitably express itself as a fragment. Paradox occurs where there is an abrupt alteration in the direction of the main axis as for example in the Gunma and Kitakyushu Art *56, 99, 61* Museums, and the Kamioka Town Hall. However much the heterogeneous character of the space and fragmentary form is emphasised Isozaki rarely loses sight of the gestalt. Wholeness is preserved. This aim is furthered by the careful cultivation of a dreamlike atmosphere which assists in drawing the distinction between reality and illusion and so enhances the fusion of disparate forms. In seeking a more flexible, tolerant, or broader consensus of form, one sufficiently strong to encompass all the variety, ambiguity, and conflict of life itself, yet retaining a common enveloping vision, Isozaki's objectives are in line with Mannerism.

Pure Form

The interment of pure forms in a constituent structure is a means of expressing the alienation of the building from its environment, and of man, from the world. Isozaki deliberately emphasises the disparity between an ideal world of pure Platonic form and an expedient, contradictory and ambiguous real world of sensible experience.

The connection of the cube and tunnel vault in Isozaki's architecture with the Western geometric design tradition, especially Renaissance theory, is slight. Instead of hierarchical centralised schemata Isozaki employs asymetrical additive arrangements of cubes along linear axes and deliberately breaks the order by running a secondary axis into the main axis in an arbitrary fashion – order is created only to be broken. The quality of arbitrariness is increased further in the tunnel vault designs by bending the form back on itself and by fashioning anagrammatic forms.

Architecture, to Isozaki's mind, is closely bound up with the transformation or assimilation of pure forms, thus:

'. . . no matter whether the process is one of returning architecture to pure forms or of transposing initially conceived pure form into an architectural context, design usually makes a round trip between these two poles. In this case, my original intention was as close an approximation of pure forms as is possible.'[35]

The cube and cylinder obtained from the square and the circle are the *prima materia* of Isozaki's later architecture. Isozaki prefers to think of the cube and cylinder as two kinds of forms which occur together instead of as an elemental binary contrast, for he writes,

'But I do not think of the cylinder as an underside or reversal of the cube.'[36]

In practice cubic additive forms and continuous tunnel vault forms are a more fundamental binary contrast of style, thus buildings are in general either one or the other, and the two imply quite distinct and diverging principles. The cube and cylinder are employed mainly as a means of establishing the basic (deep or constituent) structure. This leads to several possibilities, the units may be connected together as in the Gunma Museum and Kamioka Town Hall in an additive fashion or they may be projected as square tubes in the Oita Library and the Kitakyushu Art Museum. The origins of the cylinder and cube forms may be traced to the early development of megaskeletal form based on the sacred pillar. The symbolism of the cube and cylinder is complex. There is a need to distinguish between the reflected meaning of the cube (Japanese tradition), and the semi-cylinder or tunnel vault (classical Western

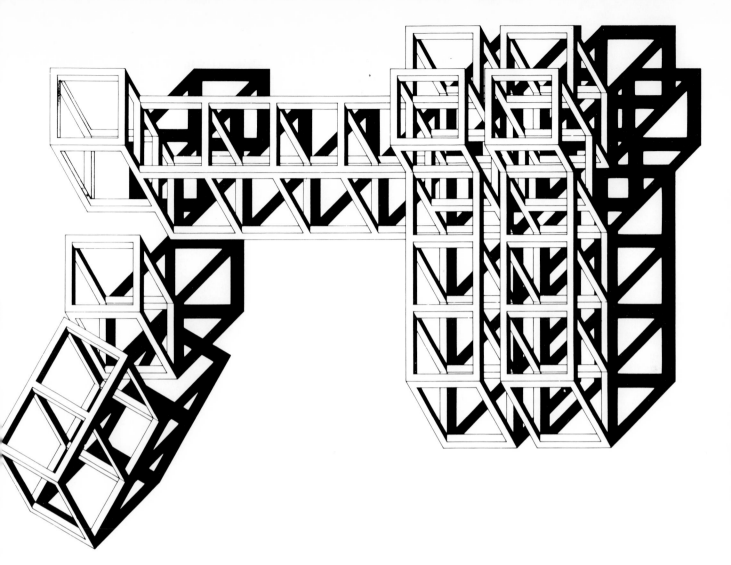

tradition), and the way in which these two primary forms are used by Isozaki. The deep structure of cube or cylinder is utterly neutral and drained of meaning, for not only do Isozaki's empty spaces fail to inspire symbolic associations, they actively discourage their formation. The neutrality and emptiness of Isozaki's spaces has its counterpart in the absence of spatiality from traditional Japanese architecture. In Japanese architecture space is non-existent; instead of 'space' there is a formless fluid openness which coalesces about columns, and is channelled by screens and walls, spreading outward through the doors and other openings. The Westerner in Isozaki's interiors is confronted by a terrifying void evoking the sensation of non-existence.

Koji Taki suggests that

'His [Isozaki's] vocabulary is entirely neutral and empty. This suggests that his square and his cube could not exist without metaphysical thought and spatial geometry. In the past, he has referred to geometry and the neo-Platonism of the Renaissance. I think this indicates a geometry that takes the lead in relation to linguistic contemplation. But the emptiest geometry is the form of his space. This does not only lead to contemplation; it is also antagonistic to it.'[37]

23 **Gunma Museum of Fine Art, Takasaki, 1971**
Diagram of the deep 'conceptual' structure for the Museum. The framework of cubes is intentionally neutral and empty

41

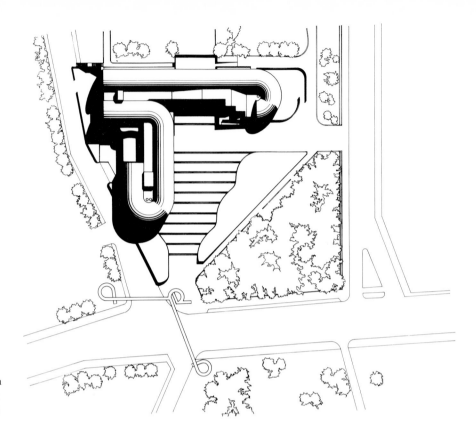

_24_ Central Library of Kitakyushu, 1972–5
The tunnel vaults of the library are bent and moulded in an arbitrary manner which suggest that they have no strength of their own and merely respond to external forces

The square is also as much a part of the Japanese architectural tradition as it is that of Europe's. The square, Isozaki writes,

'. . . has been the standard on which horizontal and vertical surfaces have been based because it was the determining element in the nature of these surfaces. Visually, Japanese architecture is replete with squares.'[38]

The cylinder appeared in Isozaki's earliest works as a metaphor for the ancient column, this vertical pillar was then rotated onto its side to create a tube expressive of a pipe for transporting fluids, thereby giving rise to a mechanical analogy. Stylistically, the tunnel vault is associated with ancient Roman vaults, Byzantine and Romanesque architecture and is an integral part of the Mediterranean tradition. Isozaki has acknowledged the European connection, singling out as influences the sixteenth century Turkish architect Mirna Siran and Andrea Palladio for his treatment of the severed end section. The portico of the Fujimi Country Clubhouse, 1974, is based on Palladio's *70, 141* Villa Poiana Maggiore, Poiana, and the end wall of the meeting room at the other end of the vault adopts the motif of the upper garden facade to the central salon of the Villa Malcontenta, Foscari. In a number of later houses, *153a* notably H's Residence, 1978, intersecting tunnel vaults are introduced which recall the cross vaults of the atrium of the Palazzo Iseppo Parto.

3
First Manner

The Pillar of Heaven

The development of architectural form by Isozaki is rooted in a single archetype, the *ten-shu* or 'heavenly column' of ancient Japanese mythology; the trabeated megaskeletal form, for example, is derived directly from the 'Pillar of Heaven', and from it stem the two branches of neo-Platonic cubic and semi-cylindrical or tunnel form. A knowledge of the origin of Isozaki's typology does not, of itself, suffice to account for the later development of form. For this, external stylistic influences namely Mannerism and Neo-Classicism, must be seen as being of equal if not greater importance. The seemingly arbitrary appearance of the works is contradicted by the presence of the sacred and spatial qualities derived from the primal form type which are a unifying factor in all Isozaki's work.

The 'Pillar of Heaven' is referred to in the 'Kojiki' (the 'Record of Things') which describes how the primal male and female deities Izanami and Izanagi, of the early Japanese creation myth are supposed to have erected a 'Heavenly Column' and then built a palace around it prior to mating. The marriage hut was meant to represent a constructed universe in microcosm with the axial shaft acting as a link that connects earth and sky at its centre. The 'sacred column of the very heart centre' (*naka-no-mihashira*) is present in the main building of the Izumo Shrine, A.D. 550, and in the Ise Shrine, built slightly later than Izumo.[1] At Ise the sacred pillar, unlike Izumo where it is far bigger than the structurally more important ridge beams, is placed under the middle of the floor of the main shrine building. The demarcation of a sacred place and the creation of space are closely related in traditional Japanese architecture. Thus the column fulfils a number of roles; it is the axis joining heaven with earth, the abode of the deity and the fundamental instrument for establishing 'place'. Moreover, a simple column placed on an empty gravel surface can arouse a sense of 'space' in the Japanese mind, especially since the sacred column is the vessel wherein the deity dwells. The column, therefore, has a significance in Japanese culture which has no equivalence in Western architecture. *Ma*, or the sense of place, is defined not by walls or solid

25a

25 **City in the Air, IV, 1962**
The exaggerated development of the
elaborate brackets is inspired by the
monumental treatment of brackets in the
Great South Gate of the Todaiji, 1199
which impart a sacred dimension to the
structure
a view of model
b plan

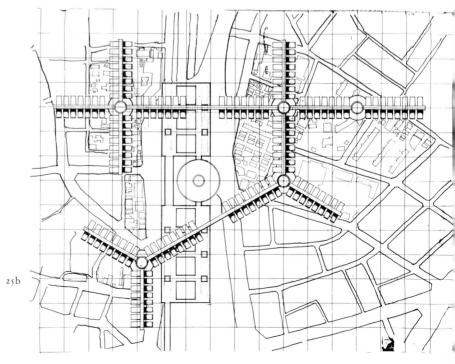

25b

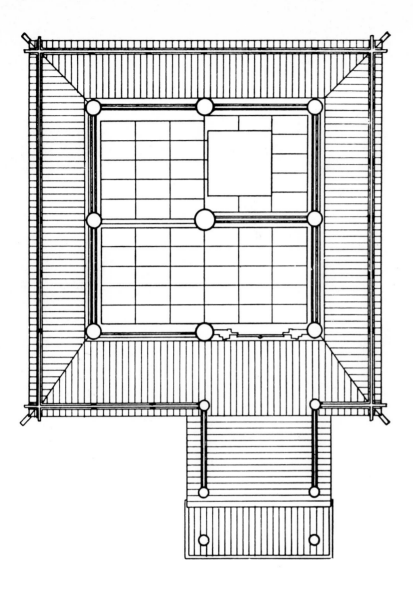

26 **Izumo Shrine, A.D. 550**
The 'sacred column of the very heart centre'
is the focal point of the main shrine

enclosures, as in the West, but by the presence of columns. The central sacred post has survived in the simple Japanese farmhouse as the *daikoku-bashira* or central sacred pillar.[2] The sacred character of the central sacred pillar is reinforced by denying it a structural role. Thus, in the tea house the pillar does not extend to the ground, nor is it customary for it to be connected to the roof support.

Isozaki transformed the primitive archetype of the central sacred pillar when he made it the basis for his invention of form. The ancient sacred dimension was obscured and overlaid by turning it on its side, increasing its scale, and hollowing out its interior so that it now becomes a hollowed-out vessel and container of human activities. In trabeated megaskeletal and tunnel form, square and semi-cylindrical tubes are laid next to one another and the

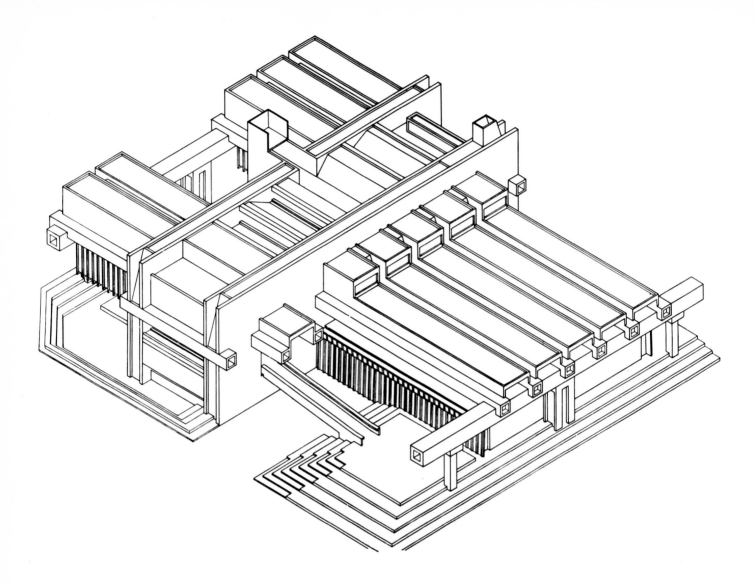

27 Oita Prefectural Library, Oita, 1962–6
Isometric. The trabeated form is achieved by stacking two sizes of hollow concrete beams one on top of the other

33b

underside left open to produce more extensive conventional spaces. In the Oita Medical Hall, 1960, the auditorium is located within a flattened oval beam; later, in the Iwata Girls' High School, 1964, the teaching spaces are formed within a series of vertically stacked beams. The Oita Prefectural Library, 1966, marks a further stage in the application of the modified sacred pillar. Here the trabeated form is achieved by stacking square tubular beams of concrete between a central spine and transverse beams supported on columns. On the outside, the end profiles imply that the interior space is made up of a number of isolated square tubes, whereas, it is evident once inside that the beam soffit has been omitted and the inverted 'U' profiles of beams used to cover a more or less open interior.

The central sacred pillar inspired a series of exploratory sketches whose importance cannot be underestimated so far as Isozaki's later architecture is

concerned. Indeed Isozaki's resuscitation of the central sacred pillar somewhat recalls Marc-Antoine Laugier's advocacy of the primitive wooden hut as the natural model of classical architecture. Furthermore, Laugier's recommendation of 'atmosphere' on one hand, and insistence on the use of elementary geometrical forms on the other, coincides to a quite remarkable degree with Isozaki's design procedures.

The immediate precursors of the hypothetical 'City in the Air' proposals are Kiyonori Kikutake's 'Tower City' of 1959, and Kenzo Tange's visionary plan for Tokyo, 1960. Kikutake's Metabolist city had hollow cylindrical cores supported on floating platforms in the sea with living capsules attached to the outside. Kenzo Tange's 'A Plan for Tokyo'[3] attempted to do for Tokyo what Le Corbusier's plan for an ideal city, 1922, had done for Paris. Tange's proposal to replace the more usual radial city structure with a linear structure,

28 **Kenzo Tange: 1960 Plan for Tokyo**
The linear structure of the Plan had a lasting effect on Isozaki's planning ideas with the result that the communal axis in one form or another is a recurring principle in his architecture

1

6

47

and the prominent post and beam expression of the megastructures forming the civic axis were an important influence on Isozaki. The Oita Prefectural Library, designed in 1962, has a structure similar to the new residential zone over Tokyo Bay. In Tange's scheme, residential halls extend outwards on either side of the commercial axis. This compares with the arrangement of the reading room, projection room, and service area, on either side of the entrance hall. Even the expressway loops bounding, and parallel to, the communal axis have been repeated in the circulation zones between double walls on either side of the entrance hall of the Oita Library. The linear scheme recurs in numerous works and is typical of former Japanese post towns.

The linear communal axis with circulation disposed on either side is a recurring motif in Isozaki's architecture, even where, as in the Oita branch of the Fukuoka Sogo Bank, none is called for by the programme. In the Oita branch the diagonal skylights extend outwards from a central spine and this pattern is enforced by an overhead gangway. Among buildings of the additive cube form type the plans of the Nagasumi branch of the Fukuoka Sogo Bank, the Gunma Prefectural Museum, the Kitakyushu Art Museum, the Oita Medical Hall Annex, and the Headquarters of the Fukuoka Sogo Bank have central linear axes. Sometimes the axis is no more than an elevated bridge, however, it is customary for it to be represented by a central public hall.

The post and beam offices on the civic axis of the Tokyo Plan were revived by Tange in 1963 in the Tsukjii Project. Isozaki's first scheme for 'City in the Air' is similar. But whereas Tange proposed an elevated orthogonal arrangement of square Kahnian cores connected by lattice girder bridge structures housing office floors in multiples of three, Isozaki's collage shows a basic span of two intermediate floors suspended on diagonal hangers between double slabs with the horizontal service runs in the interspace. Multiples of the basic span join the staggered cores. Large permanent brackets of the kind shown on the outside of the 'joint core' and the 'City in the Air', scheme were included in Tange's Communications Centre, Kofu, 1964–7. The relationship between the Shizuoka Newspaper Office Building in the Ginza district of Tokyo, 1966–7, and Isozaki's 'Joint Core' proposal is much more obvious even though the permanent brackets have been left off the outside of the cylindrical core. The cantilevered floors, nevertheless, resemble the sketches of the fourth scheme inspired by traditional cantilevered brackets systems.

Isozaki threaded the twisting office spans and cores between the ruins of a Doric temple in scheme 1 for 'City in the Air'. The intention is clear, accordingly Isozaki states in tones recalling Marinetti,

'ruins are the state of our city, and the future city will itself become a ruin one day.'

The cantilevered bracket constructions of variation 3 of 'City in the Air' investigates formal tree-like branching structures. Simplified versions of the cantilevered lattice floors in the sketches for Skopje were included in the final proposal for the city wall but instead of elevated floor spans bridging between the cores, the floors rise independently from the ground. Deprived of their structural load-bearing function the cylindrical cores contribute instead to the expressive, rhythmical character of the city wall.

The column bracket construction of variation 4 of 'City in the Air',

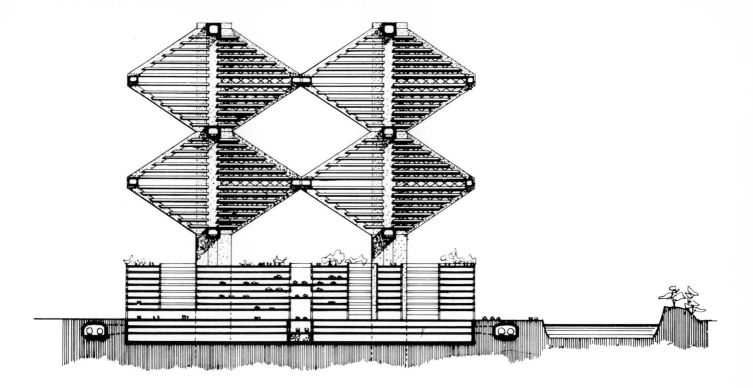

appropriated the elaborate brackets and monumental expression of the Great South Gate of the Tōdaiji, 1199. This raises an important question concerning the role of sacred expression in Isozaki's architecture, for in Japan, eave-support brackets are a sign of a god or a Buddha.[4] Bracketing occurs in sacred buildings intended as monuments glorifying a transcendental or superhuman being. In addition, the sacred, may be implied by large scale and the suggestion of strength.[5] Tange made a great play of trabeated beam forms in the 1950s and Isozaki inherited something of this in his early work. However, Isozaki went much further than Tange in giving his beams a superhuman expression, inasmuch as the process of hypertrophy is allowed to proceed to the point where instead of the beams being merely an element of construction, they now begin to include interior space. The dimensions of Isozaki's beams are by now superhuman, and the expression of strength, which for so long had been the hallmark of Japanese architecture, acquired, under the influence of Brutalism,* an unprecedented monumentality in the Iwata Girls' High School, the Oita Library and the Kitakyushu Museum of Art.

29 **City in the Air, III**
Tree-like branching structures appeared in the four proposals

*Brutalism began in England some time after the mid-1950s and was characterised by an uncompromising natural use of materials, particularly concrete, which was later allied to a Brutalism of form.

Trabeated Megaskeletal Form

The three fundamental form types – megaskeletal, cubic and semi-cylindrical – into which Isozaki's architecture can be divided are related, at least through their ancestry, although sometimes it is not at all easy to determine whether a building belongs to one type or another. The Oita Medical Hall, 1959, is the earliest example of megaskeletal form, however, it needs to be seen as the progenitor of the semi-cylindrical form type, so closely entwined are the different strands at first. Designed in 1964, the Oita Prefectural Library is the least equivocal formulation of trabeated megaskeletal form. Later examples, such as the Kitakyushu Municipal Art Museum are much less pure. The Oita Library was followed by the Fukuoka Sogo Bank head office building and the Oita and Daimyo branches, Oita Medical Hall Annex, and the Kitakyushu Municipal Art Museum. By 1972 megaskeletal form had ceased to be of such importance, since by then additive cubic and continuous semi-cylindrical had effectively become the leading form principles.

The *prima materia* of each form type are interrelated. Cubes may be created by slicing sections off the square tubes of which metaskeletal form is composed, and the tunnel vaults, instead of being square tubes, are semi-circular in section. The space beneath a trabeated roof or a tunnel roof may be fused in much the same way by aligning the open beams or tunnels side by side to form a vaulted roof. Whereas the beam elements or trabeated form are expressed in the De Stijl manner to preserve their individuality, the continuous tunnel vaults wind back on themselves or intersect with one another. The Kitakyushu Art Museum is a transitional work which combines two prominent square tubes and a plan based on squares. The Nakayama House and Clinic, 1964, while it incorporates an interesting scheme of four cubes derived no doubt from Ledoux's house for four families, lacks a clear indication of the repetitive cubic framework of the Gunma Museum of Modern Art, 1974, and Kamioka Town Hall, 1978.

The first phase – most of the early projects were executed between 1963 and 1967 – of Isozaki's independent practice, witnessed the completion of the Iwata Girls' High School, 1964, the Nakayama Residence, 1964, the Oita Prefectural Library, 1966, and the Oita branch of the Fukuoka Sogo Bank. In the years between 1955 and 1958 Tange designed several buildings with an exaggerated trabeated expression, this is most evident in the Kagawa Administration Building, Takamatsu, 1958, and the Town Hall in Kurashiki, 1960. These projects preceded Isozaki's trabeated first manner and must invariably have influenced him. The Oita Medical Hall was designed in 1959 while Isozaki was still a member of Tange's atelier and it contains the most explicit of all Isozaki's interpretations of the sacred pillar. The Medical Hall provides an important link with the burgeoning megastructure movement, though it is not properly a megastructure itself. The auditorium has been taken from a length of oval tube, and the fragment so obtained, elevated above the surrounding city on four sturdy legs. A fragment extracted from a continuous profile, both in its oval section and its derivation from continuous form, the Medical Hall is the prototype of the later series of semi-cylindrical vaulted buildings. Tange's Totsuka Golf Club, completed in 1963, is

30 Kenzo Tange: Administration Building of Kagawa Prefecture, Takamatsu, 1958
In the years prior to 1958 Tange designed a number of buildings with an exaggerated trabeated expression of the concrete, and in doing so, anticipated Isozaki's enlargement of the column and beam motif

31 Oita Medical Hall, Oita, 1960
The Hall is the earliest and most explicit statement of the sacred pillar metaphor – the auditorium is fitted inside a hollowed-out oval tube

32a

32 Iwata Girls' High School, Iwata, 1963–4
The form is similar to the earlier Medical Hall. In this instance, the classrooms are inserted in a series of vertically stacked hollow beams supported at their ends by towers. The megastructure concept called for a larger scale than has been realized
a Distant view
b section through classroom towers

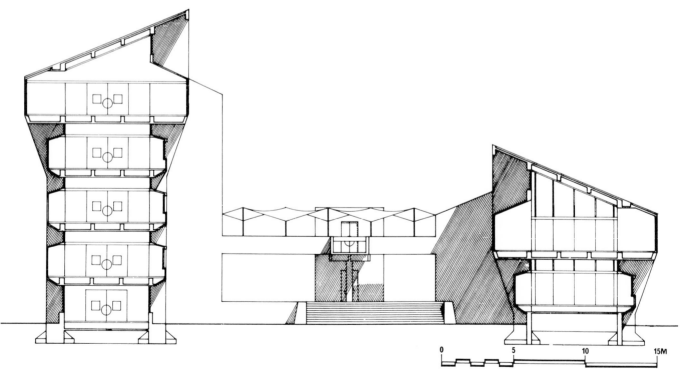

32b

reminiscent of the Medical Hall to the extent that the restaurant level beneath the suspended shell reminds one of the auditorium floor shell of the Medical Hall. Furthermore, the number of supports has also been reduced in this instance to six.

The Iwata Girls' High School is related in its expression to the earlier Medical Hall. An animal-like dimension is apparent in both, the Medical Hall even suggests a bulldog with its body supported on four stout legs. The classroom towers of the High School assume a more anthropomorphic, though none the less primitive aspect, as they confront each other across the communal axis. Only half the group of towers was completed, consequently the High School today lacks the scale called for by the megastructure concept. Certain features of the megastructure concept in the second 'City in the Air' scheme were included in the Iwata Girls' High School towers. A difference of scale and function prevented Isozaki from implementing the megastructure concept accurately. However, in one important essential the High School can be seen to resemble the second scheme; instead of laying the beam elements directly upon one another, Isozaki separated them by a narrow strip of skylights.

In these early projects Isozaki experimented with several procedures for converting the sacred pillar into a sculptural space-enfolding element; no one procedure is ever abandoned entirely, instead each continues to exercise a certain fascination. The Medical Hall points one way, the Oita Prefectural Library another. The Oita Prefectural Library is a climactic work which sums up much that has gone before, and at the same time it informs much that follows. The Library has a wider significance, for not only is it the climax of early Isozaki, it can also been seen as the culmination of a post-war tendency to give the heavy reinforced concrete frame a specifically Japanese trabeated expression. The Oita branch of the Fukuoka Sogo Bank builds upon some of the themes introduced in the Library. For example, the profile of the skylights in both buildings is the same, however, instead of being aligned *34* perpendicularly, they intersect the communal spine at forty-five degrees.

The transformation of the beam by Isozaki is extreme even for Japanese architecture; prior to the Oita Library the beam had been limited to a construction role, however, in the Library it acquired a quasi-spatial aspect. Kenzo Tange succeeded in the late 1950s in giving the reinforced concrete frame a Japanese carpentry aesthetic much as Auguste Perret had done in recasting it in accordance with classical precedent. The Kagawa Prefecture Administration Building exploited the rhythmical effect of closely spaced beams whose width is much too narrow for their depth. Tange pursued an elementarist treatment of the frame in order to emphasise the individual identity of each beam. In the Kuraskiki Town Hall the beam gained a much wider constructional significance, once the beams were laid upon one another log-cabin style to form outer walls. Isozaki took the next step in the Oita Library by giving the beam a space enfolding significance. In the Library Isozaki sought to create the impression that the building is made from large square-section hollow concrete beams laid on transverse beams on square columns. The architectural section shows that the beams are in fact open inverted 'U's. Nothing like this had been attempted before in Japanese architecture and the only precursor remotely like the Library are some houses by Paul Rudolph. The new giantism of the beams in the Library marks the conclusion of an important phase in the assimilation of beams by post-war Japanese architecture. Isozaki continued to use the hypertrophic beam, but never again was his architecture to rely so completely on it.

The Oita Library is a kind of 'balsa' architecture not so very different in its complementation of the design model as the New York Fives' 'cardboard' architecture. The simple trabeated form of the Library reflects the balsa model used in its design. The imprint of the design process on the built form, irrespective of whether balsa or cardboard is used, calls attention to the Mannerist dissociation of form and material.

20   The Library is disposed about a communal axis containing the high entrance hall, and bounded on either side by double walls, with the reading, projection and administration areas under beams supported at one end by the long core walls, and transverse beams lifted high on square columns with 27 crude column caps on the other. The roof decks on either side of the communal axis are made from two sizes of hollow square-section beams, the larger beams rest lengthwise and are separated by smaller beams. Sections of the roof have been left out, thus two small beams are absent from between the projection and administrative areas, and over the entrance access. The incompleteness of the trabeated framework is used to suggest that beam elements may be added or subtracted as needed by changes in the programme. In reality the monumentality of the heavy reinforced concrete structure would prevent any alterations being made easily. The skylights over the entrance hall incline backwards in both directions from a transverse axis at right angles to the communal axis, this axis is marked by an external stairwell.

The discrepancy between the formal constructivist expression of the outside and the interior, notably in the main reading room, points out the divergence between the simple trabeated form of the model and the built structure. On the north facade a concrete rail was introduced to complete the four sides of the square end-section of the large upper beams. This does not occur on the other side. There, the beams are stepped to provide skylights above the reading room and consequently, the beams emerge on the facade as shallow inverted 'U's supported on the smaller square-section beams. The pretended expression of the roof beams is contradicted within the building where practical considerations have modified the ideal square-tube section. The underside of both series of beams is omitted in the interior, and the two inverted 'U's thus produced are superimposed and fused. A similar scheme to the Library, even to the extent of outrigger beams is repeated in the 93 Headquarters of the Fukuoka Sogo Bank. A simplified version is also manifest 99 in the Kitakyushu Art Museum.

The strong sculptural form, rough textured concrete, even the circular outdoor seating alcoves – a motif associated with Aldo van Eyck's Orphanage School in Amsterdam – belong to Brutalism. Beams are employed, both as a structural element and as a decorative device, in such areas of the Library as the foundation walls and the entrance podium. Roofs of articulated sloping beams separated by strips of glazing appear in the Oita branch of the Fukuoka 40 Sogo Bank, and the buildings surrounding the Republic Square 1 in Tange's proposal for the reconstruction of Skopje.

33 **Oita Prefectural Library, Oita,
1962–6**
Isozaki gives the impression that the
building is constructed from hollow square
concrete beams
a View of Projection room
b Section through reading room, north
wing

33b

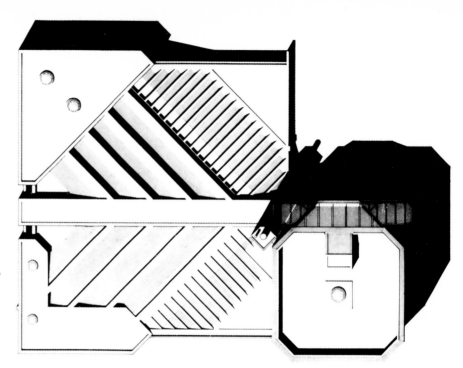

34 Oita branch, Fukuoka Mutual Bank, 1966–7
Although beam elements continued to be used, the Oita branch Bank treated them differently, in a form that is indebted to Stirling and Gowans' Leicester University Engineering Laboratories, 1963

The Oita branch of the Fukuoka Mutual Bank is a pivotal work, the design received a deal of critical attention, and in consequence, provoked a reconsideration of the established conservative image of the bank in Japan. Even more important so far as Isozaki's career was concerned, the design was greatly appreciated by an officer of the bank, Mr T. Shijima who was instrumental in having Isozaki appointed to design the new head office building for the Fukuoka Mutual Bank in Fukuoka.

The forms of the Oita Library have been reduced to a heavy scaffold of beams on posts in an effort to reinterpret the ancient archetype of the primitive shrine. Whatever may have been the conscious intention, the effect of this is to eliminate all that is superfluous until only the elemental architectural members remain. Thus, the architectural form is reduced to a few basic elements: the wall, the beam, and the column, superimposed in a simple Constructivist manner. In effect, Isozaki has sought to recover the primitive Shinto shrine in much the same way that Laugier over two centuries earlier advocated a return to the primitive hut as the true archetype of classical architecture.

Isozaki retreated from the primitive Constructivist expression of the Library in his next building, a branch of the Fukuoka Sogo Bank in Oita. The 'rusticated' concrete of the Library is replaced by smooth precast concrete panels. The sculptural composition of the Bank was inspired in a general way, by the Stirling and Gowans' Leicester University Engineering Laboratories, 1963. Such features as the diagonal glass roof and the chamfered and undercut tower have their counterparts in the Bank, however, these elements have been freely translated with the result that their relation to the original is suggested, rather than explicit. A double diagonal sloping roof similar to the Oita branch was repeated for the Daimyo branch of the Fukuoka Sogo Bank, 1968–9. In *86* the Daiymo building the two opposed roof planes are united by a transverse gallery, in contrast to the Oita solution, where a bridge on the main axis *84* reinforces the spine.

In rejecting the classical structure of space Isozaki was led to replace it by the Mannerist conception of atomised space. The Oita Bank moved on from the incomplete form of the Library to the Mannerist idea of architecture as a heterogeneous collection of separate spaces. Isozaki explained,

'While discarding the idea of parts divided from the whole, this approach also refuses to infer the whole from parts. Such treatment concentrates on the characteristic nature of each isolated "place" which is a number of separated parts.'[6]

The complex fractured quality of the exterior form is heightened in order to avoid the creation of a 'whole', and although a suspended bridge-spine assists *85* in connecting the tower physically with the banking chamber, this is insufficient in itself to bind the separate parts. The extension of beam elements of the skylights over the main business chamber and the sloping canopy of the entrance is confined to the walled enclosure.

The plan and section are arranged according to proportions derived from squares and the diagonal. Thus the lower business chamber is confined to a large square twice the size of the square base of the tower. The incorporation of simple proportions in order to relate the architectural forms is itself revealing. First, it can be seen as a return to the Renaissance practice of employing harmonic proportions, and second, it is an intimation of later neo-Platonic form. In the late 1950s the 'Cambridge School' of English Brick Brutalists showed a similar interest in the golden section, inspired no doubt, by Le Corbusier's theory of the 'Modulor'.

The unprecedented importance attached to colour in the Oita Bank[7] marked the beginning of a new formalism in Isozaki's work, and the end of the earlier, relatively brief episode of Brutalism. Colour satisfied a number of demands, it served as a form of decoration at a time when decoration was still suspect, and as such, anticipated the appearance of Supergraphics in the United States in 1968. In addition, colour saturated walls intensified the vibrancy of space. In the Oita Bank interiors colour disguised the rough texture of in situ concrete and differentiated individual spaces – this makes the building appear to be a heterogeneous collection of spatial parts.

The skeletal form of the Oita Library is so well disguised in the head office building of the Fukuoka Sogo Bank by overlaid Neo-Classical features in concert with a Mannerist heterogeneous treatment of space as to be nearly unrecognisable. The Bank is a transitional work designed in 1968 and constructed through 1970–1, it maintains the structural character of Isozaki's earlier megaskeletal phase and simultaneously initiates fresh ideas, namely Mannerist *89* space and Neo-Classical form. In place of the Library entrance hall an eleven storey slab of offices occupies the communal axis of the Bank with circulation on either side of the linear core-space. The offices are sandwiched between two blank red sandstone walls from which low wings extend outwards and are supported, in much the same manner as in the Library, by two 6 m deep

35 **Headquarters Building, Fukuoka
Mutual Bank, Fukuoka, 1968–71**
The trabeated form of the building is
overlaid by a new Neo-Classical aesthetic

outrigger beams for storing the magnetic tapes and housing the computers. The beams are connected to the red sandstone 'office wall' by steel girders *94b* turned down at their ends.

The Brutalist aesthetic of the Oita Library is replaced in the Fukuoka Sogo Bank head office, by a Neo-Classical one, inspired in part by the nineteenth century Viennese architect Otto Wagner. Isozaki has taken care to stress the formal structure of the Bank in order that the original megaskeletal character of the form is not lost. A narrow vertical gap was established between the red sandstone returns at the ends of the office slab in order to give the exterior walls the appearance of solidity, and the edge beams are similarly encased by polished slabs of red granite. The steel girders which span between the elevated beams and office walls are deliberately exposed to avoid any confusion with the longitudinal beams, and to further identify them with the building skeleton. The longitudinal beams are supported on cylindrical drums on the south and double legs on the north side where the beam is twice the width and is expressed as two beams lying side by side. Even so, the skeletal framework is somewhat obscured, so much so, that Isozaki has projected the office slab and the beams beyond the low office wings so as to indicate that the framework is not yet complete and may be added to in the future. The first floor, for example, is open on the north side where it is given over to parking, however, the open space could, if the need arose, be enclosed to create additional space for banking activities. The windows in the upper levels of the office slab are subordinated to the horizontal bands of stonework in such a way as to preserve the integrity of the wall surface.

The interior spaces of the Bank illustrate Isozaki's new Mannerist temper, for instead of representing the work as an organic, indivisible and unalterable whole, made all of a piece, the architect deliberately set about violating the unity of spaces so as to establish in its place a collection of heterogeneous spatial fragments. Isozaki explained,

'In other words, this is a conscious rejection of the universal space in favour of an aggregation of fragments.'[8]

The individual character of selected spaces scattered throughout the building is developed at the expense of the unity of the total space. Thus, four rooms in the executive suite known as 'art rooms' were entrusted to artists who designed the entire room including the walls, floor, and ceiling surfaces, as well as the furniture. Each room was considered as a total work of art, and instead of seeking to make all alike, Isozaki stressed the individual styles which set the rooms apart from one another. The intention was to emphasise the special character of each part within the building and to separate it from the whole.

Interior spaces proportioned after cubes are fundamental to Renaissance architecture; it will be recalled that Wren included a perfect cube of 40 ft for the hall of the Queen's House at Greenwich. The extent of Isozaki's break with Modern architecture is revealed by the inclusion of a white 12 m cube-space to serve as the entrance hall of the Fukuoka Sogo Bank. The hall space is *91* intersected at an upper level by a pair of narrow beams supporting a bridge that marks the communal axis. The theme of the square is repeated in the

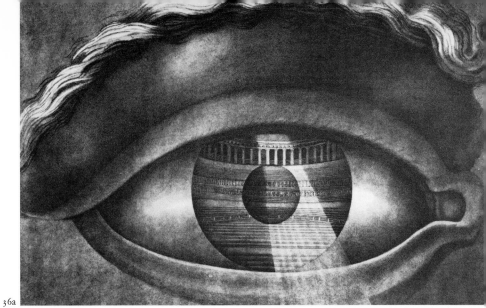

36a

36b

36c

36 **Theatre of Besançon by Ledoux**
a Glimpse of the interior
Stairwell of the Headquarters building,
Fukuoka Mutual Bank (*b* light, *c* darkened)

60

reception room in the executive suite where the image of six expanding squares covers all six surfaces of the room. The mirror-like effect of the reflected square image on all the room surfaces breaks down the boundary between semblance and reality, and being and illusion, which is a key theme in Mannerism. A similar effect occurs in the guests' dining room where a Man Ray photograph has been etched on a glass panel. When the stairwell is darkened the image can be seen reflected on both of the polished stone walls. One is reminded of the Ledoux's Mannerist rendering of the interior of the theatre of Besançon.[9] A different geometry to the reception room is used for the international conference room where silver curved screens enclosing the interpreters' booths jut out into the room and dominate the circular conference table. The surface of the booths step down and outwards in three undulating layers. Their form suggests a baroque church facade without repeating the precise convex and concave geometry, instead, the surfaces weave in and out fragmenting the tightly drawn silver skin. The interior is a brilliant mixture of machine imagery and the baroque.

90

92

37 Headquarters Building, Fukuoka Mutual Bank, Fukuoka, 1968–71
The taut silver surface of the interpreters' booths weave in and out much as does the facade of a baroque church

Around 1970, or thereabouts, the Brutalist concrete which typified Isozaki's architecture in the 1960s is replaced by smooth lustrous materials such as polished marble and aluminium panels. Isozaki's new materials recall the architecture of Otto Wagner and Adolf Loos, especially the latter who preferred rich materials treated simply to bring out their decorative quality. The change of material in the Fukuoka Sogo Bank head office and the Kitakyushu Municipal Art Museum is indicative of a radical change in Isozaki's expression of corporeal form. Thus, whereas the soundness of the early structure and its capacity to withstand external forces is affirmed by clearly articulating the components, in later works after 1970, the skeleton is debased and corporeal form is reinterpreted as components of a continuous skin stretched round the form. Consequently, the play of forces on the surface of the Kitakyushu Art Museum takes precedence over the musculature. The

95   subsequent debasement of the tectonic skeleton is assisted by the choice of a square instead of a deep beam section, and by covering the structure in square cast-aluminium panels.

Throughout the Kitakyushu Art Museum surface is emphasised at the expense of the musculature; Italian marble is used extensively for the floor and

96   upper walls of the entrance hall, and lustrous aluminium panels encase the bridges.

Rich shiny materials increase the dematerialisation of structure, for instead of a firm articulated skeleton, the corporeal form takes on the appearance of a stretched skin drawn round the forms, furthermore, these forms lack mass and any suggestion of solidity. The effect of this is to debase the structural skeleton. Instead of an active skeleton capable of withstanding external forces the building is sheathed in a passive stretched skin. The expression of corporeal form as a stretched skin leads to the introduction of undulating profiles for the interpreters' booths at the Fukuoka Sogo Bank head office and the entrance facade of the Kamioka Town Hall. Folding, stretching and even tearing the skin is a further means of emphasising its passivity. A similar feeling is excited by the arbitrary bending of the semi-cylindrical vaults of the Fujimi Country Club and the first scheme for the Kamioka Town Hall. The extreme malleability of the vaults which allows them to be bent and turned back on themselves emphasises their extreme passivity and their role as transmitters of force. By comparison, every external assault rebounds from the vigorous forms of the Oita Library.

The change from an active, assertive skeleton in favour of a passive stretched skin did not occur simultaneously with the change in spatial form. Thus the new phase in Isozaki's architecture in the 1970s appeared in each of the elements separately, rather than concurrently. The geometrical order of the Oita branch of the Fukuoka Sogo Bank is simplified in the Kitakyushu Art

99b   Museum where square projecting beams containing gallery spaces are superimposed on four square towers. The Museum space is structured by a north-south communal axis through the entrance hall; this axis is intersected

99c/d   at second floor level by an east-west axis linking the restaurant and periodic exhibition areas with the entrance hall. A system of peripheral movement between four centres within the square towers is induced by interconnecting bridges. Externally, an imposing stair proclaims the north-south communal

62

axis. The square is repeated throughout the plan and geometrical design rules the parts.

Sited astride a high ridge overlooking Kitakyushu, the Museum assumes some of the features of an acropolis. This is increased by its elevated location and monumental approach from below which produces dramatic views of the beams reminiscent of the Temple Athena Nike. The elevated position of the giant beams, and the openness of the entrance level below them, is carefully calculated to foster the impression of the beams hovering above the line of the hill. The beams have been lifted two storeys above the entrance hall and rest on transverse wings containing the periodic exhibition rooms and administration offices on either side. They seem capable of withstanding external forces, but they do not passively resist a superior force, on the

38 **Kitakyushu City Museum of Art, Kitakyushu, 1972–4**
Twin giant square beams straddle the high ridge overlooking Kitakyushu

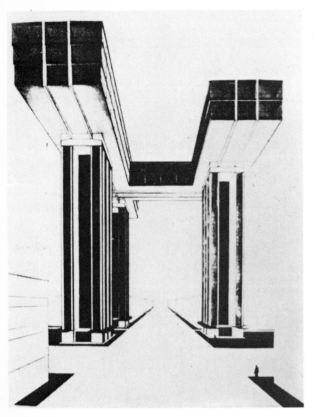

contrary, they stand triumphant and indestructible. The rusticated texture of the cast-aluminium panels covering the beams contributes to the appearance of strength. There is deliberate contrast between surface texture of the beams and their supports which are made to appear immaterial. The entrance hall is spanned by skylights much the same as those in the Oita Library, except that the Museum skylights are supported by vertical T-section beams between the two large box beams. Long roof-lights reinforce the transverse axis.

Isozaki returned to Tange's office temporarily in 1965 and 1967 to collaborate on the Plan for Skopje, and the mechanical, electrical and electronic installations of the Expo '70 Festival Plaza. The latter task enabled him to experiment with the kind of electronic media environment which, until then, had been a fantasy of Archigram and Cedric Price. Parts of the city centre for Skopje on which Isozaki worked demonstrate an assurance in urban composition which reaches a new level of sophistication. Isozaki succeeded in having a plaza, the Republic Square, included in the Plan for Skopje, and later, the 'plaza concept' was given a new dimension with the Festival Plaza of Expo '70, Osaka.

The Skopje Plan contains several examples of the first manner. Though much subdued compared with previous designs, the architecture has been reduced to simple bent beam and cylindrical column elements. Isozaki's influence is most evident in the Republic Square and the City Gate sectors where the forms reiterate themes from the Oita Library and Fukuoka Sogo Bank. The rows of towers which are separated by the cylindrical service cores of the City Gate derive from the earlier 'City in the Air' sketches. The structure of the towers is no longer the same, for, instead of the floors being supported between the structural cylindrical node, these nodes are squeezed between self-supporting lattice framed towers.

The buildings surrounding the Republic Square are reduced to three elements; a roof deck of bent beams separated by cylindrical shafts, and a tower and auditorium with splayed geometry. The splayed geometry of the tower and auditorium at either end of the plaza wall develop a motif which Isozaki first explored for the Oita branch of the Fukuoka Sogo Bank. In order to unify the plaza which is divided by the Varda River Isozaki continued the plaza wall across the river and joined its two parts by an axis. The plaza floor is extended up and over the buildings by bent-beam roof decks, which read therefore, as a terraced extension of the plaza floor. The beam, cylindrical core, and splayed masses fuse in an all embracing composition which maintains an irregular order in harmony with the meandering line of the river.

The Annex to the Oita Medical Hall does not fit conveniently into either the first or second manners, combining as it does features associated with both. In its brutal exposure of raw concrete and bent beam base storey, the Annex belongs to the first manner, yet the introduction of a stepped semi-cylindrical motif, one which is echoed in the later work of the second manner, confirms it as belonging to the succeeding phase. This is a transitional building which in the final assessment can be seen to belong to neither manner.

By 1970 the trabeated megaskeletal phase was exhausted and the second manner had begun. The Oita Medical Hall Annex is a transitional work containing features which simultaneously hark back to the megaskeletal

41 The City Gateway comprises rows of free-standing towers supported by lateral lattice structures and punctuated by cylindrical cores

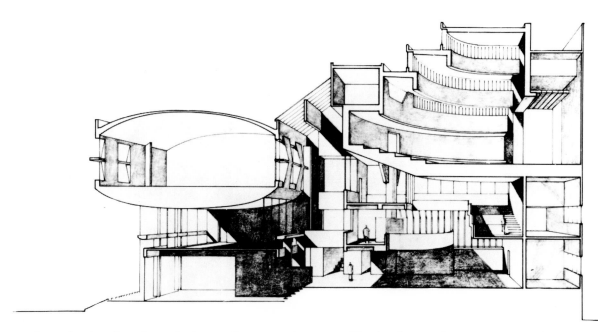

42a

mode, and point directly to the impending second manner. The fundamental element of the building is the beam, whether bent and stood upright to make a base storey, or curved to make the tiered semi-circular roof of the conference room, and not a moulded plane, consequently the Annex belongs to the first, rather than to the second manner. The Annex is a beam-building – there is a distinct absence of trabeation and two second floor columns are given an exaggerated importance – even if its semi-circular geometry and amphitheatre plan is closely identified with later semi-cylindrical schemes such as, for instance, the Kamioka Town Hall and auditorium of the Women's College, 1978.

The earlier expression of material, no doubt influenced by the surface expression of the original Medical Hall, has been continued; concrete is exposed in strong rough textured elements recalling the Brutalism of the first manner, and smooth surfaces of polished stone or shiny metal are notably absent. Even the earlier trabeated skeletal form is suppressed.

The new addition comprising a tiered lecture hall, lobby, offices and library areas is separated from the old Medical Hall by a lofty fully glazed space. The glazing continues up the sides and over the roof creating the illusion that the interspace between the two buildings is out-of-doors. Light filtering into this zone finds its way into adjacent areas.

Isozaki has explained the tiered conference room roof as having been based on the cumulus-cloud metaphor. He deliberately made the heavy concrete beams and slabs appear as light as possible by inserting continuous clerestories between each step in the roof. This somewhat unstructural arrangement is supported by a massive central spine on the outside of the roof. The spine, or

42 **Annex to Oita Medical Hall, Oita, 1970–72**
The fundamental element in this transitional work is the beam, curved in a rhythmical series to suggest a cloud formation
a section
b plan

42b

central axis, is carried over the three storey void by a bridge linking the main conference hall with the lobby which swells out on either side in quadrant-
102c shaped decks which suggest genitalia – Ledoux developed a similar imagery in his House of Entertainment – as much as cloud forms. The step motif of the roof is echoed in stepped terraces of the material and reading corners adjacent to the main conference room.

102a The rising cloud metaphor is brought to the fore externally by undercutting the conference room form and making the mezzanine transparent. The simple brutal concrete shapes of the towers at the corners and rear contradict this ethereal theme, and develop instead, an antithetical juxtaposition of solid and transparent elements more in line with eighteenth century ideas of composition.

Several historical sources have been offered for the stepped semi-cylindrical form of the conference room roof; Isozaki gives both the classical Greek amphitheatre and Palladio's Teatro Olimpico as prototypes. The former appears most likely, since, even the stage building is repeated. Regardless of the historical sources for the pattern, it is one which Isozaki has returned to in
61 his later designs, notably the Kamioka Town Hall, and the Karasima Residence, Oita, in 1978. A semi-cylindrical void was provided to serve as a
132 light well in the Sueoka Clinic, Oita, of the same year.

The Annex building is one of a group of four in the centre of Oita. The first, the original Medical Hall, was followed by a house and clinic for Dr Nakayama, a prominent local physician who had supported Isozaki's work through the years. Taken together, this group of works spans the stylistic development of the first manner, from the original Medical Hall to the Annex building.

68

4
Second manner

'Second manner' denotes works which in the main were designed after 1970. However, the two manners run parallel for a time, thus the first example of cubism, the Nakayama Residence, Oita, was completed as early as 1964. 'First manner' refers to those designs in which Isozaki freely interpreted Modern principles, 'second manner' to those in which, in the main, he struggled to free his work of inherited Modern principles. In the 'second manner' Isozaki practised a kind of 'individualism' and architectural purism based on fundamental geometrical forms such as the cube and cylinder, not unlike in many respects the anti-baroque principles of Robert Morris (1701–54)[1] and Claude-Nicholas Ledoux (1736–1806).

The relationship between Isozaki and the French revolutionary architects of the late eighteenth century arises partly because both represent attempts to develop new principles in opposition to the dominant style of the preceding period – Mannerism as an anti-Renaissance trend, Neo-Classicism as an anti-baroque trend – and partly because of Isozaki's anti-Modern kind of individualism. Admittedly, this over-simplifies the issues, nevertheless it is equally true that contemporary architecture has aligned itself, with regard to its sympathies if not its compositional practices, with periods of transition in which there is a struggle to break free of a preceding and fundamentally classical phase of development.

Change in architectural composition which is opposed to the baroque; change, it should be added, not unlike Mannerism in Italy in the sixteenth century began to appear, first in England and somewhat later in France, in countries which were remote from the sources of the new style. Whereas the baroque emphasised complex geometry and an all embracing composition, the goal now shifted from unifying the parts to one of contrasting them. In place of complex geometry, elementary geometrical solids such as the cube, the cylinder, the pyramid, and even, surprisingly, the sphere, were introduced to develop new organisations in which the independence of the constituent elements is expressed by their simple repetition, or by dramatic antithesis – a kind of composition *ad infinitum*.

In contrast to the baroque, the revolutionary composition of the eighteenth century had as its aim the concept of the independence of the individual elements. Consequently, instead of there being many weaker elements subjugated by a few stronger ones, the freedom of the individual elements within the whole was preserved – the basic idea was the independence of the parts. Emil Kaufmann referred to the new composition as 'individualism',[2] since it aimed at preserving the individual identity of the parts rather than submerging them within the unity of the whole. As early as 1742 John Wynn wrote of architecture as a 'Wild heap of inconsistent things',[3] thereby drawing attention to the contrastiveness, heterogeneous character, and independence of the new compositional form. Robert Morris advocated the cube as the cell-unit of the whole and so began the concept of cubism which was to assume such importance in eighteenth century architectural composition. Looking back, there is a startling similarity between Robert Morris's 'cubism' in the sketch showing the *Combination of Cubes*[4] and the extreme cubism of the Shukosha Building, 1978, and the Gunma Prefectural Museum of Modern Art, 1974.

Additive Cubic Form

The Nakayama Residence and Clinic, Oita, 1964 illustrates the close similarity between Isozaki's 'second manner' and the anti-baroque architecture of the French Revolution. A leading principle of that architectural revolution was the method of repetition of inorganic composition-additive form.[5] The elemental cube may be repeated at the same size, or alternately in a different size. In the second instance the presentation of one and the same motif in different sizes is termed 'reverberation'.[6] The Nakayama Residence is constructed of four 3·6 m cubes, surmounted by four additional 1·8 m cubes. The large cubes are separated by a cruciform void and the small cubes mounted over the crossing in the same pattern as the large cubes.

The connection between the Nakayama Residence and the anti-baroque compositional modes of architecture can be demonstrated by comparing its

43 **Ledoux: House of Four Families**
The motif of a cube surmounted on each corner by four smaller cubes or belvederes was taken up by Isozaki in the Nakayama Residence

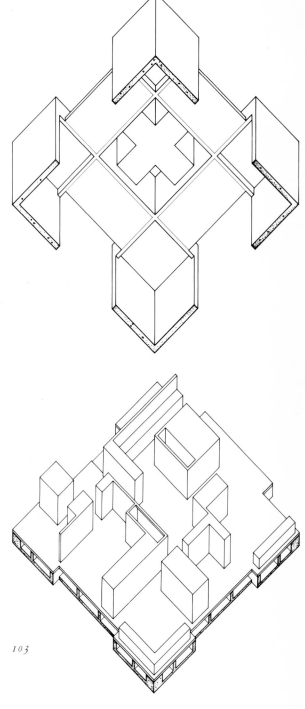

composition with two schemes by Ledoux, the Writer's House, and the House of Four Families.[7] Both of Ledoux's designs employ the motif of a cube surmounted on each corner by four smaller cubes or belvederes. In the House of Four Families this motif is repeated four times leaving a cruciform void between them. Thus, the theme of reverberating cubes is generated in the third dimension. Isozaki adopted the pattern of the four belvederes mounted on a base for the Nakayama Residence and repeated the pattern a second time over the crossing between the four large cubes, hence the small cubes which in Ledoux's scheme are belvederes become skylights. The square base is also repeated, but Isozaki required an open ground floor for the Clinic so the base is represented by projecting the thick concrete columns forward of the outer faces of the large cubes. The cruciform void between the large cubes of the first floor of the Residence is denoted by set back glass block walls.

The concentric board form-work pattern and centrality of the square window openings in the faces of the large cubes proclaim the independence of the cubes. Inside the Residence the space is structured round a central living room subdivided by a centrifugal arrangement of free-standing furniture elements to allow the interior to be changed.

Sphere and cube have been combined in the Residence for Mr A, 1968. This proposal demonstrates more clearly, perhaps than any other, Isozaki's

103

44 **Nakayama Residence, Oita, 1964**
Axonometric

71

preoccupation with female and male forms, and his reiteration of genital imagery. In most of Isozaki's projects the image of the male genital organ is disguised rather than explicit as in Mr A's Residence. Isozaki explained the symbolism of the house in the following manner:

'The sphere was chosen for the shape of the bedroom because it symbolises the womb, but the form is in addition another primary material to be fitted into the cube. This is a stable house because the sphere is attached to the ground on the side on which it is fitted to the cube. The mobile house moves like a trailer and is subject to blowing-up (pneumatic). The fixed is female, and the mobile is male; this metaphor is one of the characteristics of the form.'[8]

Isozaki is surely not the first to introduce genital forms into architecture; Ledoux did so in his House of Entertainment, as also did Jean-Jacques Le Queu in the Sanctuary of the Creator. The inspiration for Mr A's Residence is uncertain, however it is worth noting that Ledoux designed a Shelter for Rural Guards in the shape of a sphere.[9] However, instead of lowering the sphere in a sunken basin, Isozaki raised it up and suspended it between the four corner columns of the 7·2 m cube. Ledoux's sphere, containing stables on the ground floor, the bedrooms and kitchen on the main floor in the centre, and storage above, was reached by four bridges. Isozaki, as he emphasises in the previous quotation, stabilized the sphere by connecting it to a cube. In another scheme for a cemetery, Ledoux embedded the sphere in a base for *17* stability. The mobile male compartment of A's house has been given a phallic form replete with two transparent pneumatic testicles which enclose the entrance hall, air-lock, kitchen, and bathroom. This section of the house is mounted on a truck and thrusts against the side of the cube. The cube is itself made of a rigid frame with pneumatic membranes stretched between them and

45 **Ledoux: Shelter for Rural Guards**
The shelter is in the shape of a sphere

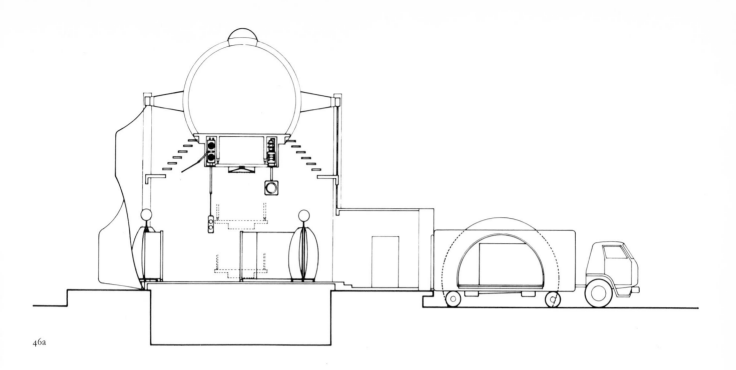

46a

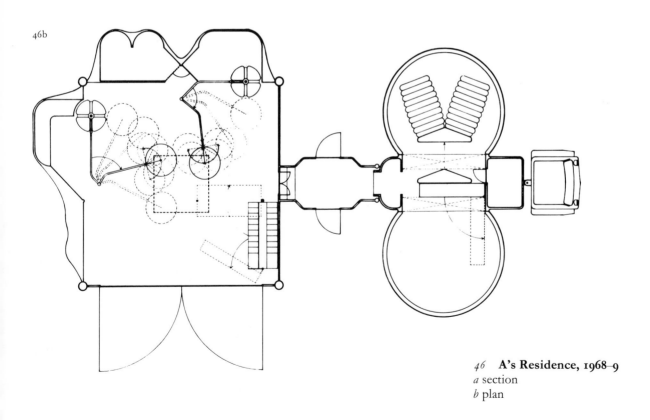

46b

46 **A's Residence, 1968–9**
a section
b plan

47 **Festival Plaza, Expo '70, Osaka,
1967–70**
The Festival Plaza represented the most
advanced application in terms of both
technology and scale of the electric circus
entertainment facility envisaged by
Archigram
View at night.

74

deformed in erotic protusions. Mobile screens subdivide the open interior of the cube which is dominated by the underside of the womb-sphere. One thing which emerges from all this is the manner in which Isozaki has interpreted the communal axis of Tange's linear urban structures in terms of a biological metaphor, namely the seminal tract. The erotic imagery of Isozaki's mobile house contrasts with the hard 'machine' styling of Kisho Kurokawa's capsule housing. This points to an essential difference between the two; Isozaki is fundamentally uninterested in technology, whereas Kurokawa, until recently, derived his aesthetic from the process of industrialism.

The geometrical motif of cube and sphere was extended to the performing robot of the Expo '70 Festival Plaza; this remarkable giant sported two spherical control booths on a rotating armature above a cube-shaped trunk which housed a dressing room and an assortment of gadgetry for collecting and emitting information. Light, sound, smoke and bubbles also poured forth from large tubes in its sides on pulsed instructions. The mobile sub-control station comprised a cube shaped upper section mounted on a tower for activating lights, sound and trolley equipment.

In his work on the equipment for the Festival Plaza Isozaki married the geometrical purism of Ledoux with the idea of replacing architecture by 'servicing', as a means of liberating man from the past. Two distinct traditions, the Italian piazza, and the modern film and television studio, are combined in Isozaki's electric piazza. Similar facilities existed indoors; indeed, the Cedric Price and Archigram proposals were little more than a belated attempt to catch up with, and assimilate, established film and television technology within the realm of architecture. This was a clear case of the *avant-garde* chasing technology.

The very act of realising the concept out-of-doors and on unprecedented scale, transformed the nature of the idea, inasmuch as the attempt to abolish architecture led to its replacement by equally intrusive machinery. Whereas Archigram envisaged a kind of open-air circus made up from balloons, travelling cranes, robots and light/sound equipment, or buried it underground in their Instant City, and Monte Carlo Entertainments Building proposals of 1969, the Expo '70 equipment and enclosure were found to be much more substantial, and this in turn created new opportunities for a second elevated piazza in the space frame roof.

105 The Festival Plaza was envisaged in 1966 in the early stages of planning Expo '70, but it was not till 1969, the same year that Archigram published their Instant City and Monte Carlo projects, that the detailed design was finalised. The origin of Tange's magnificent (108 m wide × 291·6 m long × 37·7 m high) space frame canopy is unmistakable. However, Tange quickly ascertained a non-monumental membrane structure suspended from balloons, as proposed by Archigram in their Instant City scheme, was impractical. He ensured, nevertheless, that the canopy with its 10 m × 10 m pneumatic polyester cushion cover was made as visually light as it could be.

The Festival Plaza equipment, as it was realised, not only fulfilled aims of the Monte Carlo Entertainments Centre proposal, but, in the event, advanced some distance beyond them. By comparison, Isozaki ventured into new territory which Archigram could only dream about in their collage fantasies.

It is ironical that at the moment when Archigram was on tenterhooks over the possibility of building their Monte Carlo scheme, Isozaki was busy finalising the details for a much larger and complex open air circus for a mass Expo audience.

The performing robot is a parody of the 'Mickey Mouse' image, whose two *104* distinctive circular ears are repeated in the rotating control room spheres on the armature above the body of the robot. The robot stands on four legs and has arms which can be extended from the cube-shaped trunk as required.

In his series of houses for the people of an ideal city, 1773 – and the *barrières* or toll houses, 1785–9 – Ledoux focussed his imagination on the elaboration of a selected theme. The possibility of exploring a building type such as a house, toll house, or in Isozaki's case, branch banks, in a series of theoretically related designs obviously fascinated Isozaki. Not surprisingly, the performing robot of the Festival Plaza turns out on examination to have been inspired by one of Ledoux's toll houses, the Barrière de Montmartre.[10] Isozaki's branch banks for the Fukuoka Sogo Bank and his barrel vaulted houses belong to a similar theoretical series as Ledoux's designs. The Fukuoka Sogo Branch Banks at Nagasumi and Ropponmatsu are just such essays in cubism. They demonstrate two alternative responses to the anti-architecture drive to do away with monumental skeletal forms, which, in the final assessment, are the expression of the Mannerist need to create a spiritualised, dematerialised, disembodied form. In these works Isozaki seems to have abandoned as unattainable his aim of conveying his feelings and thoughts in a non-material media. The two Fukuoka Sogo Branch Banks, in common with the extraordinary Festival Plaza, seek a dematerialised architecture, one that is freed from material. Dematerialisation is furthered by imposing the metaphor 'twilight' on both banks, something the revolutionary French architects of the eighteenth century would have described somewhat less pretentiously as the creation of atmosphere, and by the imposition of a Cartesian grid on all surfaces, both inside as well as outside.

48 **Ropponmatsu branch, Fukuoka Mutual Bank, Fukuoka, 1971–2**
The street 'face' – the vents serve as eyes – is covered with a tensed skin of squared aluminium panels which are carried around the round corners

The debasement of the architectural skeleton of the Ropponmatsu branch – the simpler of the two – is accomplished by overlaying the exterior with a thin stretched skin of square aluminium panels whose continuity is emphasised by carrying them round the rounded corners. The square grid is taken inside, where square grey painted plywood panels are used for walls, and crimped wire-netting is suspended in square panels below the roof and the second floor. The structure is hidden from view by an identical square grid which is imposed over all the interior surfaces. Even the lobby seating is square.

110

The street facade of the Ropponmatsu branch is symmetrical and comprises two squares, each six panels long, laid side by side and bordered by a strip a half panel wide on the corners and a one panel deep band at roof level. The symmetry of the two prominent circular vent-eyes increases the extreme frontality of the facade. A conference room and staff amenities are situated on a wide central bridge over the main business floor; this permits the interior space to rise up on either side till it bumps against the roof. An austere grid is imposed over all surfaces and everything from the metal handrails, structural steelwork and doors to the partitions.

108

The plan of the Nagasumi branch, the first of the duo to be completed, is nearly identical to that of the Ropponmatsu branch. There is one difference, however, the two side wings extend forward to the street forming a rectangular court for parking between them. The plan is, once again, a square seventeen by seventeen modules from which the forecourt has been subtracted. The square theme is continued in the main glass facade which is again subdivided into two squares each six panels wide, (7·5 m × 7·5 m). A smaller second floor on the same lines as the Ropponmatsu branch is separated

49 **Nagasumi branch, Fukuoka Mutual Bank, 1971**
Perspective. The mass of the bank is dematerialized by the extreme imposition of a square grid throughout

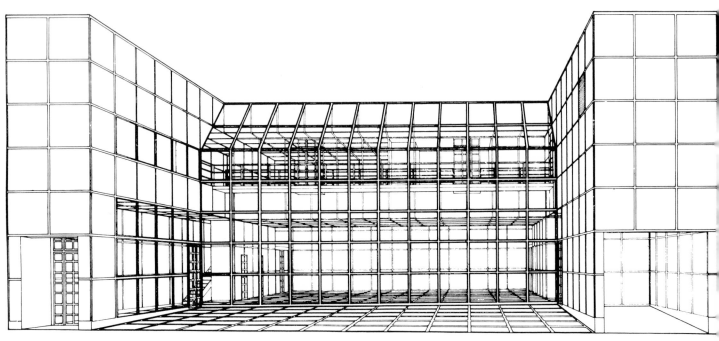

from the outside walls by a full height space three modules wide. The materials used in the interior are the same as the Ropponmatsu branch except that the panels are painted a pale blue to accentuate the lack of contrast, and increase the indeterminate atmosphere of 'twilight'. Isozaki's early drawings of the Nagasumi branch affirmed the elementary geometrical character and transparency of the grid surfaces which appear to extend to infinity – composition *ad infinitum*.

In Isozaki's architecture, an intellectual outlook is allied to the most pervasive of Mannerist intentions, with the result that rational form is parodied by dissonance, erosion of form, duality, displacement, and the tension evoked by juxtaposed cubes. The Saga branch of the Fukuoka Sogo Bank is possibly the most interesting of the series – it develops the geometrical theme of two displaced cubes. Both the Ropponmatsu and Nagasumi branches incorporate two squares in their main facades. In addition, four cubes make up the Nagasumi branch. The design for the Saga branch is based on a primary oblong block nine units square and twenty seven long, from which the middle cube (9 × 9 × 9 units) has been subtracted leaving two identical cubes facing one another across the void left by the absent cube. Subsequently, the right cube is displaced forward four units on plan. This enabled Isozaki to introduce the diagonal motif from the earlier Branch Bank at Oita. The final form of the solids is obtained by subtracting unitary cube elements from the main cubes (9 × 9 × 9 units) in a procedure which results in the erosion of the primary forms thereby reducing them to the status of incomplete forms. It is significant that Isozaki chose to subtract unitary cubes from the primary cubes instead of assembling them additively from the

107

112a

50 **Saga branch, Fukuoka Mutual Bank, Saga, 1973**
Perspective. The form of the bank is based on two offset cubes

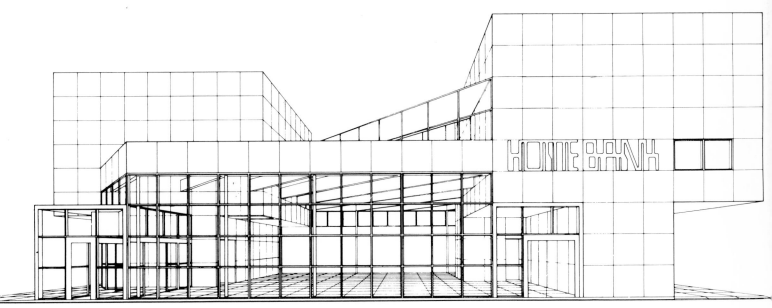

111

112b

smaller cubes; this is consistent with his intention to express the building form as a fragment. A square grid is applied to all the surfaces; thus the floor is covered with a black and white checker pattern, and the main cubes are encased in a jacket of polished white marble. The selection of materials, glass, and white marble, is typical of second manner preferences, which lead to an undermining of the sense of reality and enhanced ambiguity. The staggered arrangement of the two primary cubes results in a distorted central space which is then covered by beams set at forty-five degrees. The diagonal lines of the ceiling increase the discord between the displaced cubes.

Again, if one looks to Ledoux, his House for Two Cabinetmakers, and House for Two Merchants,[11] pursued a similar composition of oblong blocks and superimposed smaller blocks. On reflection, however, the solution to the problem of combining two independent blocks presented in the House of the Modiste, and the House of Two Artists,[12] comes nearest to the final composition of the Saga branch. But, whereas Ledoux adopts a symmetrical arrangement, Isozaki chose an anti-classical pattern of diagonally displaced cubes.

Isozaki designed two country clubhouses, one for Fujimi (1972–4), near Oita, and another for Katsuyama (1973–4) which was never built. The designs were in contrasting form types; a moulded tunnel vault was adopted for the Fujimi Clubhouse, unlike the Katsuyama project, which was conceived as an undifferentiated array of juxtaposed cubes. The Katsuyama scheme was created by removing six cubes from a square assembly of sixteen cubes, four on each side. Isozaki omitted the six cubes from one corner in a forty-five degree symmetrical pattern, and then superimposed four transparent cubes a half level (one storey) above this cubic framework. The resulting composition is an incomplete square in plan with a sawtoothed diagonal edge facing the view. The cubic framework of the main floor is interpenetrated by four elevated cubes, offset a half length.

51 **Katsuyama Country Clubhouse, 1973–4**
The conceptual structure is composed of ten cubes surmounted by four additional cubes
a conceptual diagram
b plan

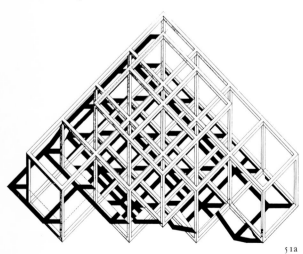

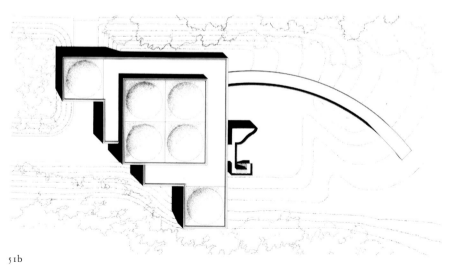

51a   51b

The second floor, directly below the skylights, is penetrated by a high space bordered on one side by a balcony shaped according to the standard Marilyn Monroe profile. Opposite this, a circular bridge slices through the building into the central space in an all too explicit collision of geometry. Stylistically, the Katsuyama Country Clubhouse was designed with concrete domes similar in shape to Aldo van Eyck's Orphanage School, Amsterdam, 1958–60. The staggered pattern of Aldo van Eyck's School has been preserved in the Katsuyama scheme by omitting a corner from the primary square.

At the bottom of the treatment of form of the Gunma Prefectural Museum of Modern Art, 1970–4, is the unvoiced question regarding the problematical nature of external reality, and the sense that the inner world of man's spirit is more fundamental to man's humanity. Isozaki seems to be asking through his architecture and the Gunma Museum in particular, which is more important, the universe of the spirit, or the world he finds about him? For, often as not, material things of the world turn out to be illusory, whereas, dreams and fantasies are found to offer a more reliable indication of the human situation.

The ideal neo-Platonic character of the Museum, sited on an almost flat section of the Gunma Plain, south-east of the cities of Maebashi and Takasaki, was intensified until it comes to resemble an architectural apparition. Everything about the Museum, from its simple additive composition of independent cubes, to the reduplication of the square grid over all its surfaces, contributes to the dematerialisation of the building form. The dematerialisation of form in this, and other works, is inspired by more than an anti-architecture mistrust of the monumental; it reflects, and indeed, chronicles the mounting spirituality of Isozaki's work. If it is impossible to create architecture without at the same time employing materials, then, Isozaki asks, cannot one make buildings which are transparent, appear to lack mass, and float? The aim is to deny architectural forms any more substantial reality than that of a mirror image. The mirror is a recurrent theme in Isozaki's architecture: the polished stone facing of the stair of the Fukuoka Sogo head office, and the much larger grand stair of the Gunma Museum, are used to reflect images of Man Ray's 'eye' in the former, and the stair itself in the latter. The ambiguity of experience is questioned further in the Gunma Museum by juxtaposing a parody of the grand stair next to the real stair. Here, Isozaki asks the semantic question: what does 'stair' denote, in what respects is the parody not a 'stair'?

The plans of the Kitakyushu and Gunma Museums of Art are similar; but whereas the grand stair and entrance axis are fitted between two giant beams in Kitakyushu, the central axis of the Gunma Museum is bounded by two

53

52 Gunma Prefectural Museum of Fine Art, Takasaki, 1971–4
Perspective, conceptual structure. The Museum was conceived as a pure Platonic scaffold whose very emptiness recoils from the creation of semantic value

53 Parmigianino: Self Portrait from a Convex Mirror, Kunsthistorisches Museum, Vienna
The mirror is an important idea in 16th century Mannerism where it is used to question reality. Mirror surfaces recur in Isozaki's architecture

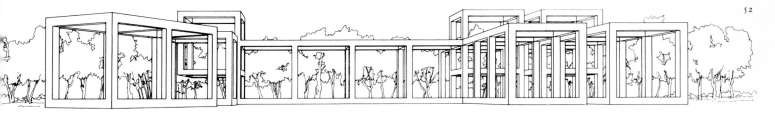

52

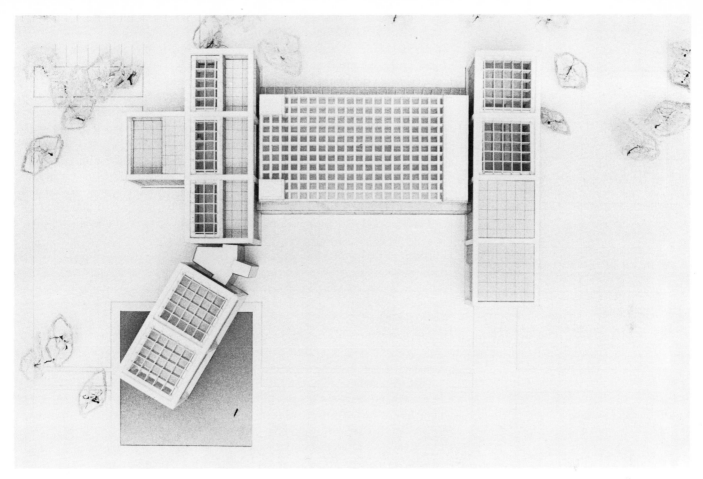

rows of cubes, and a loosely connected wing on the left side is tilted towards the secondary axis in violation of the basic geometry. The Gunma cubes press in on and constrict the entrance hall in contrast to the much larger pseudo-grand stair located in the lobby next to it. The constriction of the real stair is contrasted with the openness and freedom of the pseudo stair. The external entrance stair – a transcription of the Spanish steps – is much larger in the case of the Kitakyushu Museum where the entrance hall, which is such a prominent feature, is displaced to the side of the central axis in the Gunma Museum of Art.

In an early design, published in 1972,[13] Isozaki showed two north-south blocks of four and three open cubes, containing the entrance hall and lobby, and gallery with storage, connected by a low central gallery. Two cubes, housing the sculpture court and traditional Japanese art, were loosely attached to the left block and angled over a square ornamental pool. The sketches do not agree with the model, for the drawings show the two cubes enclosed on the second floor by glazing; the model has them infilled by aluminium panels set back from the faces of the frames. In the completed

54   **Gunma Prefectural Museum of Fine Art, Takasaki, 1971–4**
The polished stone walls enclosing the staircase produce new images which become confused with the real stair

83

building the structure is hidden beneath a taut skin of aluminium panels, so it is impossible to see how the loads are carried by the frame. Moreover, the structural skeleton appears to be of a uniform section regardless of the stress function or the imposed loads.

A second row of five cubes was added in the executed design on the east of the entry axis to complete the symmetry of this block and three rooms constructed within the three southernmost cubes to accommodate a restaurant, offices and library. These recall the four Doric columns of the conversation pit of Charles Moore's 1962 Orinda house, or else are a reminder of the primitive Shinto shrine. Such cubes within cubes draw attention, much as does the play within a play, to the different levels of reality in the same work. Which is the real room, the large cube or the post and beam enclosure within it?

The stepped platform at the end of the lobby offers the visual paradox of mutually contradictory perspectives, the actual perspective of the passageway leading to the studio is opposed by the false inverted perspective of the platform which converges towards the observer. Isozaki has resorted to familiar Mannerist devices to debase the meaning of 'stair', thus by distorting the scale of the steps of the marble platform he has disqualified it as a 'stair', yet in nearly every other respect the platform is a 'stair'. In some ways the sham grand stair – possibly because of its grandeur, prominence, placement and the openness of the landing above – is more convincing than the real stair which is constricted and arbitrarily terminated by a circular Corbusian stair that juts out from nowhere. These counterlogical devices – the enlarged scale and inverted perspective of the pseudo-grand stair, the constriction and the spatial incoherence of the termination of the real stair – are all part of the Mannerist repertoire that sets out to invert convention and undermine objective reality. The Mannerist tendency to depth, and the paradox of the juxtaposition of two compelling categories of space, is exemplified by the extreme elongation and confinement of the main entrance corridor which is contrasted with the spaciousness of the lobby adjoining it. The entrance corridor bores deeply into the body of the block, parting the two rows of cubes much as Mannerist painting tends to develop pictorial space in depth instead of in breadth.[14]

The desire for spatial continuity and spatial coherence, which was such a feature of Modern architecture, gave way in the 1970s to spatial fragmentation and the expression of different spatial values within the same building. Instead of the same geometrical order being maintained throughout the building, multiple geometries are frequently included. The dissonant angle of the independent wing, containing the Yamatane collection of traditional Japanese art, is intended, by its transgression of the fundamental geometry, to draw attention to the special status of the collection.

Space is atomised in the Gunma Museum of Art and little effort is spent on harmonising the individual spatial values beyond enhancing their contrastiveness. Sometimes links are developed between spaces as when the converging lines of the stepped platform in the lobby are extended over, and on to, the stair beside the browsing area on the second floor, or the ramp at the end of the main central gallery is used to relate the gallery space to the upper exhibition room.

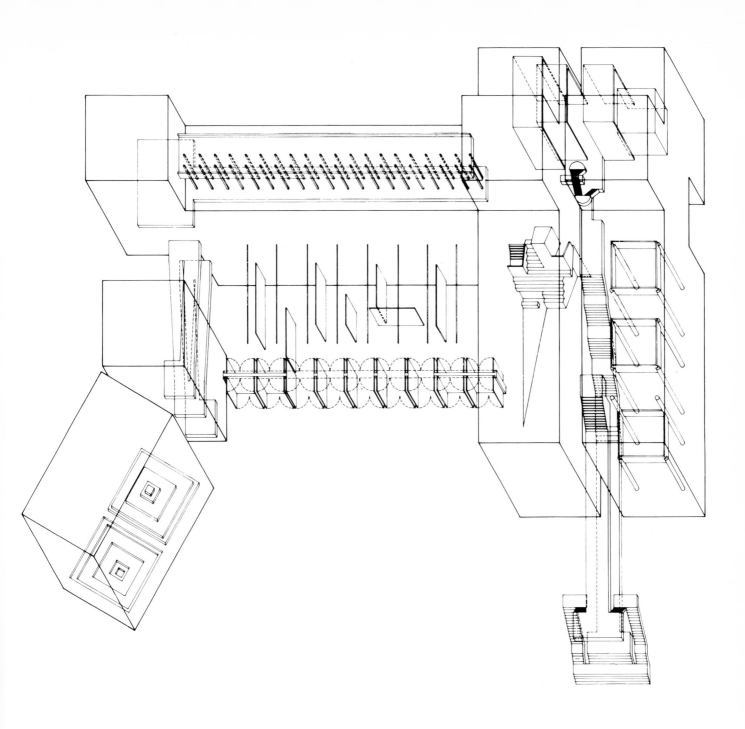

56 Analytical drawing of Gunma Museum
indicates the heterogeneous nature and
complexity of the spatial form with rooms
within rooms

The outside of the Museum of Art is covered with standard square panels of gleaming aluminium, or where this does not happen, it is glazed according to the same grid. Half panels are used to turn the corners, in the same fashion as the Ropponmatsu Branch Bank, so as to ensure the continuity of the stretched metallic skin. The ideal neo-Platonic expression of the exterior increased its abstraction and remoteness from nature. The most striking feature of the Museum is its isolation from its background; it is as though Isozaki wishes to emphasise the irreconcilable antagonism between his building and its environment.[15] The repetition of the facial end elevation from the Oita Medical Hall on the end of the Yamatane Wing implies that the antagonism is really one of man and his surroundings, and of civilization and nature.

116

113

In the Shukosha Building, Fukuoka, 1978, Isozaki broke with Neo-Classical precedent and based his composition, not on Ledoux's cubic forms, but the Tzara House of 1926–7, by the pioneer Modernist Adolf Loos.[16] The context of the Tzara House is quite different from that of the Shukosha Building, yet Isozaki has maintained the same number of floors, and an almost identical main facade – he even repeats the exterior treatment of the Tzara House which rests on a solid base of squared masonry. The stepped terraces at the rear of the Shukosha Building have their counterparts in the Tzara House. The Tzara House possessed the added attraction, besides its association with Loos, in that Tzara was a prominent Dadaist, and this must have recommended itself in respect of the parallels between Dada and Mannerism. Moreover, the travertine facing along the base of the long walls has been deliberately 'split open' to suggest that the building is on the point of failure – a conceit worthy of Giulio Romano – and the semi-circular entry confronts the visitor with six false doors, in addition to the two real ones.

The Shukosha Building, unlike the Tzara House, which was designed as a private residence with a separate apartment, accommodates a lecture room, library, saloons, show rooms, and offices, as well as gallery space. A penthouse was provided on the roof directly above the lift shaft. Isozaki replaced the large saloon and terrace in front of the Tzara House on the fourth floor by a double height space and mezzanine.

The conceptual structure of the Shukosha Building is based on a framework of six identical cubes, in two superimposed groups of three, the lower group being sheathed in travertine to contrast it with the transparent volumes of the upper series of three cubes. The penthouse above the main block is similarly composed of six smaller cubes. Isozaki also relied on two eighteenth century principles, the antithesis of solid and void of the base and superimposed series of cubes of the main block, and the principle of reverberation – that is the presentation of one and the same motif in different sizes – in the cubic structures of the main block and the small penthouse, and the rear terrace.

The main facade of the Shukosha Building has a number of features in common with the Tzara House; the splayed recess is echoed by the semi-circular entrance niche, the two windows on level three are also repeated, and even the wide balcony recess has been echoed by the open *piano nobile* of the upper cubes. Isozaki transferred Loos' original motif,[17] giving it a facial aspect, the doors have become teeth – false teeth – and the two windows in

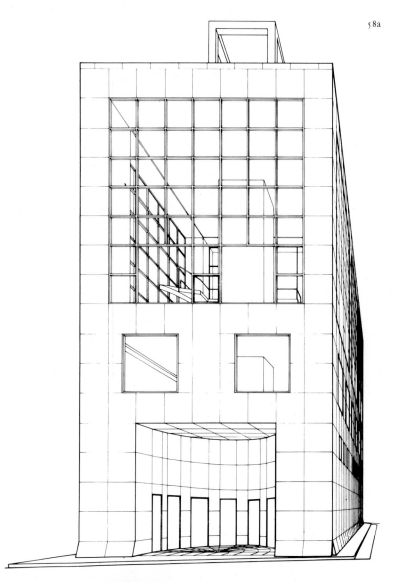

58a

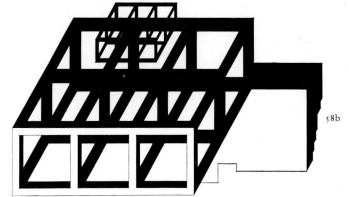

58b

57 **Adolf Loos: Tzara House, Paris, 1926–7**

58 **Shukosha Building, Fukuoka, 1974–5**
a Perspective
b Conceptual structure

turn represent eyes. And once again, Isozaki poses the semantic question of what constitutes a door, what qualities distinguish an actual door from a display window made to resemble a real door?

As befits an Art Gallery, the Shukosha Building has been given the form of a Renaissance palazzo,[18] it even has a *piano nobile* of sorts. However, unlike the Renaissance palazzo the main floor of the building is on the fifth floor. Throughout the building, space is atomised inasmuch as 'the cube establishes a region for the aggregation of fragments existing without interconnections.'[19] Style is itself the programme, for it is apparent that Isozaki has been inspired less by the programme than by other works of architecture, notably the Tzara House. Furthermore, the interior of the clients' room on the fifth floor is treated as a total work of art in much the same fashion as the 'art rooms' of the Fukuoka Bank Head Office.

A bridge – by now the bridge has become almost a mandatory feature of any Isozaki building – is provided on the second floor with convex balconies that swell out on either side in a similar fashion to the entry axis of the Oita Medical Hall Annex. Much of Isozaki's skill has been focussed on the clients' room where the white lift shaft is debased by an indeterminate array of blue, yellow, green and tangerine graphics which spill over onto the circular stair, balcony, air conditioning ductwork, and floor edge, adding to the ambiguity of these forms. Colour is used to fragment form and to blur the boundaries between

120

59 **Shukosha Building, Fukuoka, 1974–5**
a Tokonoma
b Stepped block, enclosure, President's room
The stepped block here and in the Gunma Museum serves as a modern representation of the traditional Japanese Tokonoma

elements so that their separate identities are no longer clear. The clients' room, separated from the lift by a glass screen, is extremely formal; at the opposite end to the lift, the space is dominated by Aiko Miyawaki's stepped block enclosing the president's room and toilets. The stepped sculpture takes on some of the traditional significance of the Tokonoma alcove[20] for displaying flowers, a painting, or a piece of calligraphy. Unlike the Tokonoma, however, which permitted all kinds of pictures to be hung without disrupting the tranquillity of the main space within the room, the stepped sculpture has a definite object character which intrudes upon the space of the clients' room.

This is the second time Isozaki has used the device of the pseudo-stair as a sculptural motif, but, unlike the Gunma example, some of the steps of the Shukosha block are translucent and can be illuminated from inside.

Cube and Cylinder

Around 1975 Isozaki began experimenting with a mixed geometry in which he combined cubes with large circular walls. Mixed cube and cylinder geometries occur in the Kitakyushu Municipal Exhibition Hall, 1978. But, whereas the circular wall is the leading motif in the Kamioka Town Hall, in the Kitakyushu Exhibition Hall it is merely a subsidiary one appended one end to a repetitive composition of stacked cubes. The Sueoka Clinic, Oita, 1978, employs the novel idea of an upright semi-cylindrical space inserted within the body of the clinic. A similar scheme to that of the Kamioka Town Hall reappears on a much reduced scale for the Karasima Residence, Oita, 1978. Here a circular glassblock wall is included within an incomplete cube whose outline is suggested by free-standing side walls which have been continued up to the street frontage. The combined cube and cylinder motif is of long standing in classical design: examples of semi-circular porticoes can be found in such schemes by Ledoux as the House with Belvedere and the House with Balcony.[21] Indeed the Kamioka Town Hall is largely a recapitulation of this Neo-Classical motif.

The Kitakyushu Municipal Exhibition Hall is one of Isozaki's most lyrical works, yet on the surface it appears, perhaps because of the repetitive character of its form, to be one of his most cerebral. Isozaki stated

... 'I am convinced that at least 90 per cent of architectural design must be logical. Without logical content it is impossible to build under the current conditions in Japan. For that reason, I always try to maintain a common quality that is the support of the current age. Without a mass of logicality, of course, there would be no transgression because there would be nothing to transgress. I believe that one must first create and use the 90 per cent mass of logicality and then, add to, or extract from it, a few things that do not harmonize.'[22]

The repetitive character of the exhibition structure and the standard masts, from which the roof is suspended, appears pre-eminently logical; where, one asks, are the transgressions of which Isozaki speaks?

The Exhibition Hall is on the Kitakyushu waterfront, adjacent to a pier, surrounded by warehouses, cranes, and a steel works. It appropriates several images, all of which are connected with the sea: it has the plan of an oil tanker – there is even a rounded bridge – the roof system of parallel skylights is inspired by the image of sunlight flashing on the surface of water, and the mast

60 **West Japan General Exhibition
Centre, Kitakyushu, 1975–7**
The maritime industrial setting of the centre
has been paraphrased in the mast and cable
structure which supports the roof

structures reflect the stayed mast silhouette of sailing clippers.

The cube, rather than the circular wall, is the leading motif of the *124* Exhibition Hall. An outer wall, or barrier, of stepped white cubes is ranged along the long sides of the hall, and serves as a base for the roof columns. This Neo-Classical stepped base is contrasted in colour with the ship-grey wall of the hall itself and the roof structure. The pattern of the cubes has been *122* continued in the square grid of the glazed screen which enables the north end of the hall to extend visually into an enclosed court. Sheltered behind the circular street facade, and on the opposite side of the court, is a restaurant. One of the delights of the roof structure is the subtle definition of the *123* triangular spaces beneath the inclined back stay cables. The Neo-Classical treatment of the base structures neatly complements the aggressive engineering expression of the roof structure. This engineering expression is reinforced by the structural details which are extremely fine and relate well to the architecture.

The outstanding feature of the Exhibition Hall is the hall space itself. This *12* ought normally to have been dull and oppressive, but the semi-transparency of the glazed beams creates an atmosphere filled with soft filtered daylight. Instead of a heavy lid, the roof overhead sparkles and dances in the sunlight. Isozaki has succeeded in extracting the maximum of poetic imagery from what might have been one of the most pedestrian of buildings; the Exhibition Hall excites memories of the sky over the sea, and the cable-stayed mast structures of sailing ships. This unassuming Exhibition Hall is one of Isozaki's most outstanding works.

The stretched skin of the Kamioka Town Hall is drawn so tightly over the *128* plane east facade that it begins to tear and curl in long convex and concave strips that became entangled in the sixteen cube framework of the adjoining block. The play of invisible forces on the continuous surface of the building has become so intense that the passive skin is rent. Kamioka Town Hall marks an important stage in the debasement of corporeal form. Up till then the skeleton had been covered by a continuous skin, but at Kamioka that skin develops fissures under the action of great tension. This process is confined to the entrance, or east facade; on the west side, the two cylindrical facades are unaffected by the drama of disintegration going on behind them.

The Kamioka Town Hall is located in a narrow valley in mountainous Gifu *65* Prefecture. So great is the contrast between the dazzling aluminium panels and its pure geometry, and the surrounding jumbled dark timber and iron roofed houses, that the Town Hall appears completely isolated from the city. Three geometries are combined in the Town Hall. Thus, two powerful semi-cylinders are welded symmetrically to a rectangular block; the lower one swerves past and through it to circle around the paving on the opposite side and on the north end an independent group of eight cubes abut the main block. The axis of this group has been rotated 22·5 degrees, and the exterior clad in stone to distinguish it from the main block. The cylindrical terraces have horizontal strips of glass block and the main hall is glazed above the lower terrace, thereby establishing a motif of three circular walls, with the upper and lower walls separated by a smaller portico of columns behind the glazed wall.

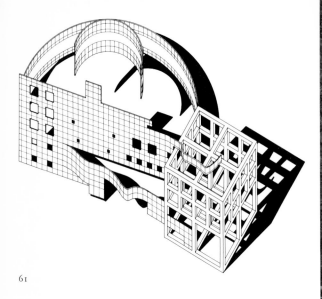

61

61 Kamioka Town Hall, Kamioka, 1978
Conceptual structure. The form is a
heterogeneous one in which the major
theme of symmetrical semi-cylindrical
screens is contrasted by an eccentric cube-
block

62 Set in a narrow valley in mountainous
Gifu Prefecture the pure geometry and
dazzling aluminium skin isolates the Town
Hall from the surrounding houses

63 Kamioka Town Hall
a first scheme
b final scheme

62

63a

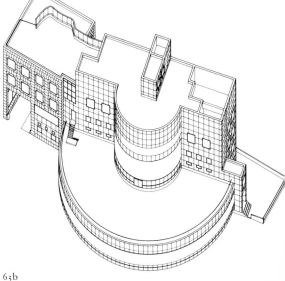

63b

In the early stages Isozaki proposed three parallel vaults, one larger than the others, and connected by an inclined glazed roof,[23] but this idea was abandoned in favour of the classical portico scheme of the completed building. Something of the character of the circular classical temple peristyle is present in the semi-circular colonnade, extending through two storeys, of the main hall. Isozaki gives the daring geometry of Ledoux's 'Oikema' as the source of the semi-circular lower terrace and indicates that the end pavilion of the Town Hall is a simplified temple. A comparison of the two projects shows little direct similarity, except perhaps for their architects' shared passion for seeing buildings as aggregates of simple geometrical shapes. The curious classical appearance of the symmetrical semi-cylindrical facade is oddly matched by the 1920s usage of glass blocks for the horizontal bands of the semi-circular walls.

The council chamber is situated within the smaller of the semi-cylinders, directly above the offices on the main floor. The upper and lower semi-cylindrical forms are connected by a transparent wall of glass, through which can be seen the semi-circular colonnade of the main hall; in doing this Isozaki consciously contrasted the upper and lower solids with the slender intermediate void.

Throughout the interior each space is given its own distinct identity: the council chamber with its stone faced bureau strikes an extremely formal and dignified note, elsewhere the spaces are more relaxed and pastel greens and yellows begin to appear. Several rooms have stepped recessed ceilings similar to ones designed by Fumihiko Maki for the Toyota Memorial Centre.

Returning to the outside, the main block is covered with shiny aluminium panels. In contrast to the Gunma Museum, the windows are no longer anchored within the square grid, but overlay and interrupt it. The windows of the displaced temple-wing are isolated from the granite facing by wide aluminium frames. A section of the curved Marilyn Monroe band has been continued past the column and into the first bay of the end pavilion, thereby linking it with the main block. A second curved aluminium strap breaks away from the main facade and carries over the roof of the end pavilion forming a walled court. The Kamioka Town Hall is a curious and complex demonstration of Isozaki's high Mannerist style.

Provided its Mannerist inclinations can be kept in check, the new style, like Palladio's aesthetic, is extremely adaptable. The return to a more classical form, and simple geometry, permits the architect to give even quite ordinary buildings a degree of style. The Sueoka Clinic, Oita, 1978, shows how the form of a modest suburban clinic can be made stylish in a Neo-Classical way without becoming pretentious or overdone.

Once again it is possible to establish parallels between the semi-cylindrical light well in the centre of the four cube group and such schemes by Ledoux as the House with the Cylindrical Crowning and the Second House of the Lumberman.[24] These two designs have a cylinder wedged between the belvederes which disrupts the unity of the whole. Furthermore, the tripartite division of the facade of the House with the Cylindrical Crowning is echoed in the Sueoka Clinic. Ledoux divided his wall into an open colonnade and open belvederes which he contrasted with a blank intermediate storey. The same

130
129

64 **Sueoka Medical Clinic, Oita, 1978**
Axonometric. The clinic is stylish in a Neo-Classical way without becoming pretentious or overdone

127

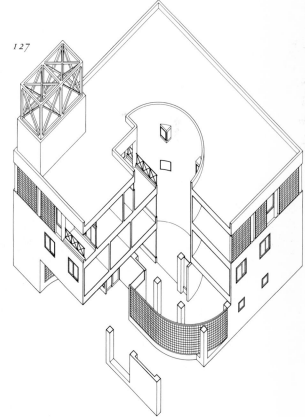

contrasting surface arrangement is repeated for the Sueoka Clinic where the S-shaped wall of the *porte-cochère* opened up the ground floor; above this the glass block walls of the doctors' apartments on the third floor are separated by a blank brick wall punctuated by square windows. Glass block walls and lights in barrel vaults became a characteristic feature of Isozaki's work in the late 1970s, inspired to some extent by the rediscovery of P. Chareau's maison d'Alsace. Emil Kaufmann wrote his book *Von Ledoux bis Le Corbusier* in 1933, in which he argued that Le Corbusier was the foremost exponent of the great transformation during the eighteenth century. It should not come as a surprise, therefore, to find in the Sueoka Clinic oblique references to the Villa Savoie. The interior of the Clinic is modest and practical; on the ground floor the semi-circular wall of the light well sweeps around the core drawing the space with it.

133

The geometry of the Karasima Residence, Oita, 1978, is related to Kamioka Town Hall, and to a lesser extent, to the Sueoka Clinic. This small two storey house is square in plan with a semi-cylindrical core that rises through the second floor and is expressed externally. The cylindrical wall rests on a cubic chair at the front that encloses the entrance. This semi-cylindrical hall is filled by an articulated stair between the first and second floors and is lit by a deep band of glass blocks. Two widely spaced square windows, a central door and threshold represent a not too abstract face on the street facade.

In the late 1970s, the boundary between cubic and cylindrical form becomes increasingly vague and difficult to define, especially where, as in his transitional works, Isozaki contrasts cube and cylinder.

Continuous Semi-cylindrical Form

If Claude-Nicolas Ledoux is the chief inspiration for additive cubic form, then Étienne-Louis Boullée supplies the leading historical antecedent for Isozaki's elaboration of continuous cylindrical form. For in analysing the historical sources of each mode it is apparent that a single design by Boullée, the Library Hall, was decisive. The principal compositional element of the design is a large barrel vault. A tremendous tension develops from the contrasting arrangement of such units as colonnades and the book stacks, and the barrel vault. Isozaki gives Palladio and Ledoux's Saltworks as specific references for the Fujimi Country Clubhouse but these must be considered as secondary to the Library Hall.

Within the range of neo-Platonic forms Isozaki seized on two, the cube and cylinder, as contrasting types, and to a considerable extent he maintains the two types as separate form categories, except where he develops a hermaphroditic type combining characteristics of both, such as in the Kamioka Town Hall.

The limpness and passivity of Isozaki's vaults is a universal factor, since the lack of an independent resisting skeleton expresses an essential characteristic of tectonic corporeal form of the 1970s. Isozaki's choice, therefore, of a

134

pneumatic envelope for the Computer City, 1972, scheme is symptomatic because the tension in the membrane of a pneumatic structure is produced by the difference in air pressure acting on the membrane. Nothing could express

65 **Boullée: Royal Library**
Interior. The design was an important
influence on Isozaki's adumbration of the
barrel vault in such works as the
Kitakyushu Library

better than this example the essential passivity of the building's skin. The
corporeal forms have become transmitters of force, where once, in Modern
architecture, the skeleton was an active generator of force. In later works the
flaccidity of the barrel vaults is conveyed by moulding them in the shape of a
question mark – in the Fujimi Clubhouse – or other equally arbitrary patterns.
In his discussion of the corporeal forms of the second phase of post-medieval
architecture Paul Frankl describes a similar condition:

'The [corporeal forms] are not in a position to assert themselves freely. They are incomplete
fragments of an unending association of physical forces. The volition that works within them is
always so controlled that it is opposed to a stronger force. They groan under this burden or
seem to be thrown into a passionate rage against it. We face these corporeal forms as men who
are incapable of controlling our fate, dissatisfied with our lot, but unable to alter it.'[25]

Isozaki's barrel vaults have been deprived of any will of their own and can
only submit meekly to the pressure of external forces.

It is appropriate to begin this discussion of cylindrical form with the Yano
Residence because it combines a vertical cylindrical surface such as is
encountered in the Kamioka Town Hall, with the much more usual barrel
vault. There is also a separate clinic besides the house, the two being sited on a
beautiful hillside near Kawasaki in Kanagawa Prefecture south of Tokyo.

The primitive hut archetype is a recurring idea in Isozaki's work. It would
simplify matters if Isozaki's explanation of the Yano House in terms of the
cylindrical Broker's House by Ledoux,[26] or even the opposed cylindrical
forms of Le Corbusier's Villa Adriana[27] were adequate, yet there is something
quite primitive about the form which these sources fail to explain. One is

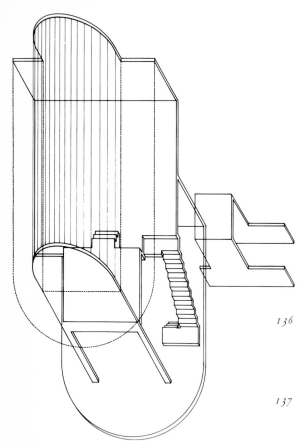

66 Yano House, Kawasaki, 1975
Schematic diagram: the house is composed
of two opposed semi-cylinders one within
the other

136

137

138

struck by the elevation of the lower vertical cylindrical wall which evokes the facial features of a clay *haniwa** figure. It is also true that even though the barrel vault is identified with western Mediterranean architecture, there is also an ancient connection with Japanese tradition. Saddle-shaped roofs were typical of the *haniwa* dwellings for nobles and Tange elected to commemorate this house type in the hyperbolic paraboloid shaped arch of the Hiroshima Peace Memorial. The earlier Yayoi high floor dwelling included an elevated platform reached by steps or a ladder directly under the roof. This arrangement has been repeated in the Yano House where the main bedroom and study are positioned on a raised platform beneath the barrel vault.

It is difficult to see the connection between the Broker's House and the Yano Residence, except perhaps in the way in which Ledoux contrasted each element which in turn strives to assert itself. In the Yano Residence the vertical cylinder is opposed by the horizontal barrel vault and the two forms are mediated by a cube over the dining area which supports the roof. The isolation of the building from the environment is increased by the closed form of the barrel vault which effectively confines the interior space except at the ends and isolates it from the surrounding landscape which is especially beautiful.

The low caseworks and partitions separating the bedroom and study terminate below the springing of the barrel vault to allow the space to race back and forth under the vault. Rather than isolating the upper level from the ground floor, the study floor is depressed below the roof to permit views down into the living room and out to the surrounding woods through a narrow slit on the east side of the study. A smaller cubic volume within the living room is implied by two free-standing cylindrical columns. This open cube confronts the larger semi-cylindrical volume of the living room perforating the ceiling and carrying the space through and up into the opposing barrel vault. Isozaki increased the 'emptiness' of the living room by depriving it of furniture except for two bare globes on either side of the central window. The living room spills out diagonally on either side of the longitudinal axis through stepped openings leading out-of-doors. The white painted concrete contrasts with the landscape, isolating the house on the hillside.

Three major public commissions, the Fujimi Country Clubhouse, 1972–4, the Kitakyushu Central Library 1973–5, and the Oita Audio-Visual Centre, 1978, separate the Yano House from a later series of barrel vaulted residences including H's House, 1979. At first glance, the articulation of the pliable barrel vaults may seem unduly arbitrary, yet common principles may be inferred from these works. The barrel vault, unless it is a rising vault such as the Romans sometimes employed, is inflexible and limited in the shapes of spaces that may be enclosed. It is unsuited to irregular compact plan shapes, and ideally should be applied to continuous uniform spaces of hall buildings. In order to adapt the barrel vault to the requirements of divers plan shapes, Isozaki has had to double back and fuse his vaults so as to form wider amalgamated spaces. The Fujimi Clubhouse comprises a single continuous

*Haniwa are clay cylinders, sometimes decorated with plastic figures.

96

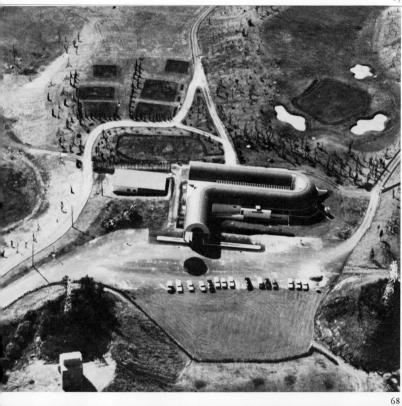

67 **Fujimi Country Clubhouse, near Oita, 1972–4**
The vault is doubled back on itself in a seemingly arbitrary fashion to increase the depth

68 **Central Library of Kitakyushu City, 1972–5**
The Library is based on two crooked vaults which start together and then separate

68

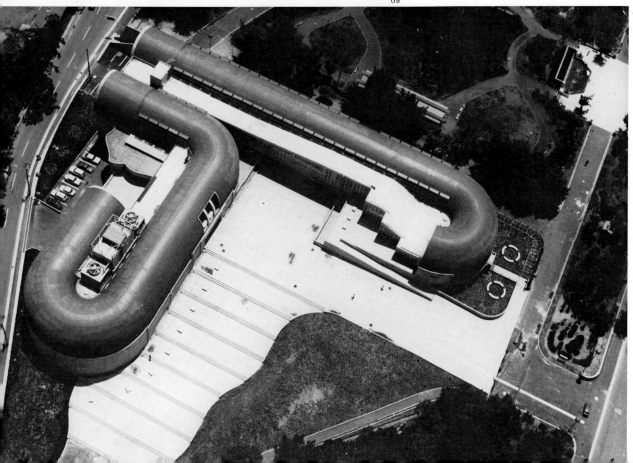

69 Oita Audio-Visual Centre, 1978
The identical vaults are ranged in parallel

vault turned back on itself and ending in a right-angle elbow. The Kitakyushu Central Library has two vaults, one straight and crooked at its end, the other advancing a short way in company with its fellow then diverging at right-angles and ending similarly in a crook. The Oita Audio-Visual Centre is a double-barrel form. The two parallel vaults issue from a square auditorium and are separated by a continuous skylight over the central hall. Infill elements are provided in the two earlier schemes to enclose additional areas outside the barrel vaults and to create bridging spaces between the vaults.

Of all Isozaki's buildings, the Fujimi Country Clubhouse near Oita is the most Palladian. It comes closest to realizing the ideal Palladian villa. Isozaki's recreation of the Platonic archetype is imbued with sophistication and witty allusion, but a detailed comparison instantly reveals the historical references to Palladio's Villa Poiana Maggiore and Malcontenta to be more implicit than real. Isozaki is more concerned to draw attention to such relations than he is to studiously repeat the specific Palladian motifs. The two end sections of the severed barrel vault preserve the traditional wall treatment of solid pierced by vertical openings with a central emphasis and balanced subsidiary accents on either side, but the specific patterns of these important elevations can only be seen to resemble the Palladian original in a general way.

Nevertheless, in a subtle way Isozaki manages to recall the essence of the ideal Palladian villa. The barrel vault roof of the clubhouse – a joke on the golf

145

70 Palladio: Villa Poiana Maggiore
Palladio is an important influence, along with Ledoux, In Isozaki's second manner.

club metaphor – is raised above and suspended over the main lounge and dining hall on the second floor which is placed on an elevated base that isolates it from the landscape. The isolation of the building from its setting is increased by the white stucco walls and the fluid whale-like humped shape of the barrel vault. Isozaki chose to express the Western origin of golf, and such associations as leisure and rural gentility, by giving it a Palladian form, yet his evocation of the Palladian villa lacks the precision a Scottish castle would have given it. This vagueness points to the real intention behind the Palladian theme which is to evoke the Platonic archetype of the ideal villa and convert it into a picturesque object in the landscape in order to express the antagonism between the absolute and the arbitrary, the abstract and the natural, which is so central to Mannerism.

The lounge on the second floor is fused to create a single space where the barrel vault curls back on itself. The treatment of the barrel vault is equivocal: on one hand, Isozaki expresses the roof as a plane transparent ceiling and emphasises the horizontal dimensions by the stainless steel ties between the edges of the vault, and on the other, he draws attention to the fluid curvilinear character of the tunnels which channel the space around the interior by inserting a skylight between the paved vaults. The cross-section through the vaults reveals the discrepancy; the lounge is spanned by two 4·8 m radius barrel vaults separated by a 2·4 m gap. The interval between the adjacent vaults is concealed by a skylight strip which simultaneously defines the

71a

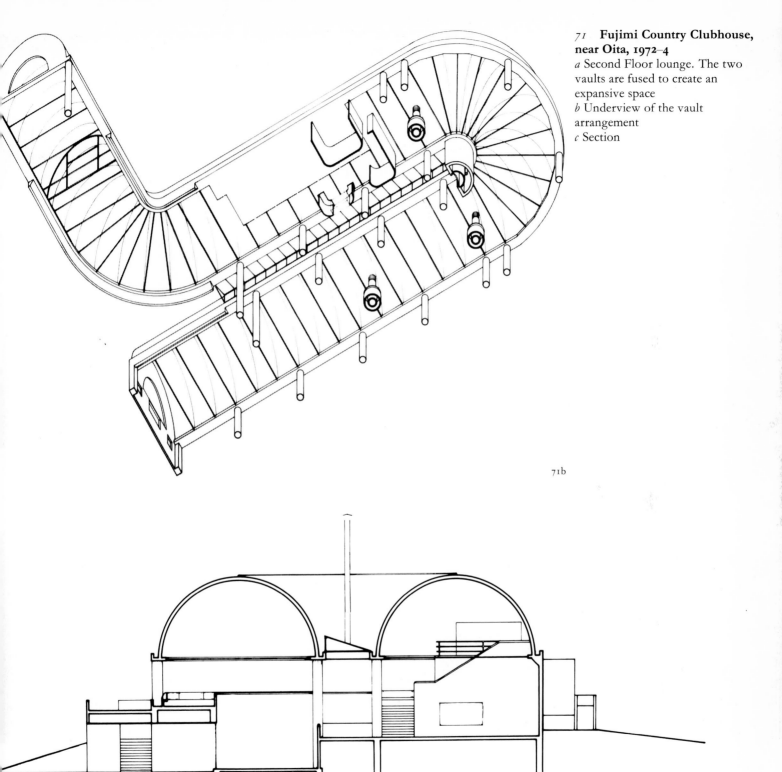

71 **Fujimi Country Clubhouse, near Oita, 1972–4**
a Second Floor lounge. The two vaults are fused to create an expansive space
b Underview of the vault arrangement
c Section

71b

71c

72 Ledoux: House of the Surveyors of
the River

curvilinear movement of the vault while it reinforces the horizontal
dimension of the lounge space. The ends of the vaults are stiffened by inside
flanges and this results in their expression as thick tubes rather than as shells,
consequently the image of the ends of the vaults, especially the entrance *porte-
cochère*, is closer to Ledoux's House of the Surveyors of the River[28] than it is to
the arched shapes of Palladio's facades.

To some extent the uneasiness in the handling of the clubhouse tunnel vault
arises from the difficulty in matching the vault pattern with the plan. This led
Isozaki to suppress the spatial character of the semi-cylindrical vault which
reads as a dimensionless white void lacking structural strength.

The copper covered vault is raised up on minimal cylindrical-section
concrete columns and the opening between the wide sill-beam of the vault and
the base storey of the clubhouse has been infilled by continuous strip
windows. The windows add to the transparency of the second floor and allow
uninterrupted views of the golf course. The idea was for

'a building that was a semi-cylinder undulating and skimming across the ridge line of hills'.[29]

In other words, an open pavilion with its interior spaces orientated to the
surrounding landscape.

The metaphor of a giant whale, which Isozaki assures us he intended for the
curved end of the vault,[30] may seem somewhat unsuited to the image of a
floating vault – considering its bulk – however, this points to the animal-like
quality Isozaki sought to give the building's serpentine vault.

The interior from the walls and underside of the tunnel vault to the floor
covering is white, the only exceptions are the stainless steel ties of the vault –
their shining surface may have been intended to minimise their intrusion but
has the very opposite effect – the bright red band of ventilation under the
windows and the doors, and the equally bright yellow air conditioning outlets
which double as cloak racks. The end wall of the vault blocks and abruptly
143 terminates the flow of the space. The windows in the wall frame views of the

outside; the central square one reveals views of the surrounding landscape while the semi-circular one above it admits the sky to the interior. On passing *142* through the entrance visitors are directed by the semi-circular curvature of the vault to the main space where one staircase leads upwards to the dining room and another, next to it, leads downwards to the lockers on the first floor. The movement does not coincide with the strong pull of the vault and confusion results. Nevertheless, both as an exercise in style, and as a piece of architecture, the Fujimi Country Clubhouse must rank as one of Isozaki's most successful works.

The uniform section of the barrel vaults of the Fujimi Clubhouse and the Kitakyushu Library allowed repetitive construction methods to be used, thus the Fujimi vault was poured in place using movable forms, unlike the Kitakyushu vault, which was assembled from standard precast concrete ribbed elements split in two at the centre. The methods used in their construction have an important bearing on the appearance and spatial character of the finished vaults. The absence of contrast in the white Fujimi vault produces a light open space which spills out through the open sides, in contrast to the heavy exposed concrete vaults of the Kitakyushu Library which are carried down to the floor. The resulting vault produces a closed tunnel-like interior whose form is delineated by the rhythmical lines of the ribs as they swing round bends in the tunnel. The Kitakyushu vaults recall decorative Gothic vaulting. The ribs of the vaults revert surprisingly to the skeletal articulation of corporeal form which was more typical of the first manner.

The treatment of the vaults of the Kitakyushu Central Library derive their impetus, if not their form, from Boullée's design for the Royal Library.[31] It is *65* hardly an exaggeration to say that the regular arrangement of the transverse ribs and the secondary longitudinal stringers echo the texture of Boullée's coffered barrel vault. But beyond this, very little else has been imitated. Boullée provided an enormous skylight along the centre line of his vault; Isozaki lights his interior from openings along both sides of the Kitakyushu vault. To have followed Boullée's intention would have meant ignoring structural logic, and would have resulted in an excessive contrast of light. Boullée's Library is divided in three zones: the lower zone of receding stepped bookstacks, and intermediate zone of Ionic columns, and the lofty zone of the coffered barrel vault. Isozaki's vaults rise directly from the floor, thereby *148* eliminating the two lower zones in Boullée's scheme; consequently, the interior of Isozaki's Library is dominated by the monolithic barrel vault. This is divided, however, at least in the reference rooms on the second floor, into an upper solid vault, an intermediate strip of windows, and a lower solid band. In the exhibition area the vault is completely solid. Irrespective of their differences, Isozaki manages to express much the same point of view as Boullée and those other revolutionary architects – that of form for form's sake.

The heaviness of the Kitakyushu vaults is accentuated by the pattern of the ribs. If the Fujimi Clubhouse was conceived as a light open pavilion looking out on the landscape, then in direct contrast to it, the Kitakyushu Library is an introverted cave utterly isolated from the world around it. These two

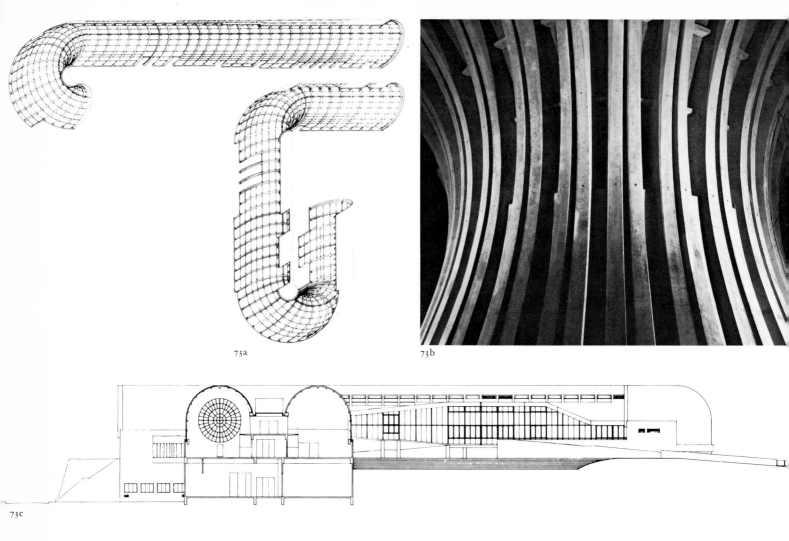

73a

73b

73c

**73 Central Library of Kitakyushu City,
1972–5**

a Diagram, precast concrete vault   *68*
b Corner detail
c Section

buildings demonstrate Isozaki's flexibility in being able to convey diametrically opposed meanings using nearly identical means.

The deliberate juxtaposition of the two competing vaults invests the composition with considerable tension. Since this begs the question, which is the dominant vault, which is subordinate, to which the answer is given, neither one. In order to overcome the unduly restrictive uniformity of the vault spaces Isozaki was forced to fragment his form and return the vaults in a hook form. Fused double vaults cover the children's library and the history museum exhibition hall – this is separated from the main library by the entrance and terrace off the Marilyn Monroe shaped restaurant. The greatest tension occurs in the 'void' between the two vaults. This common space is not emphasised or given the same significance it has in the Fujimi Clubhouse, instead the two vaults are treated as separate forms.

Isozaki further fragmented the form by including conventional infill structures for the children's library lobby and ramp, and between the vault of the history museum. As well a crude Marilyn Monroe silhouette, heavily *16* framed in concrete, produces marked dissonance. The awkwardness of the restaurant is less evident once inside, but regrettably, the stepped glass wall lacks the necessary fluidity required to convey some of the seductive appeal of the real Marilyn Monroe. On the eastern side of the broad stepped approach to the library the grass covered mounds spill over the paving, attacking and eroding its edge in a series of bulges which echo the sensuous lines of the star. At the meeting of the paving and the mounds, one encounters once more the *24* favourite Mannerist theme, that is the antagonism of culture and nature, and man and his surroundings. This antagonism has been represented by contrasting the closed, almost claustrophobic interior and geometrical forms of the two displaced tunnel vaults with the open plaza. Furthermore, the Mannerist tendency to depth has been satisfied by the prolonged perspective of the extended ribbed vaults.

The Oita Audio-Visual Centre was completed late in 1978, and whereas one of the two parallel vaults of the Kitakyushu Library is displaced, the two vaults of the Audio-Visual Centre maintain their parallel disposition. In the *69* Kitakyushu Library the central ramp on the south side of the library vault is placed over the communal axis and the museum vault displaced and bent to its final hooked form. The physical location of the ramp is used to suggest the original parallel double vault configuration which is the basis of the final vault form. The principle of displaced vault forms was continued in the first scheme for the Kamioka Town Hall which comprised three parallel vaults; of these the lower one of the three was deflected and turned outward.

The powerful cannons of the Oita Audio-Visual Centre are directed away from the street and fire into the void beyond. Consequently, instead of pointing forward the barrel vaults are directed away from the front of the building and in the opposite direction to the covered entry ramp. The opposition of the building and entry ramp axes introduces a functionless dimension which is typical of the irrational Mannerist treatment of form.

The influence of Stirling's later work and Leon Krier can be detected in the austere Neo-Classical arrangement of the mixed forms, especially the highly self-conscious design sketches for the project. These show Isozaki, his back turned to the viewer, admiring his building.[32] The Centre is assembled from a mixture of geometrical solids which reverberate in the building form. Whereas, the barrel vault has been reproduced without any alteration in size, the triangular profile glass canopy and the square auditorium at the front of the Centre are repeated at different sizes elsewhere in the building: the canopy recurs over the central hall in the cleavage between the barrel vaults, and the auditorium reappears in a cubic water tower at the end of, and between, the two vaults. The triangular section of the entry canopy is opposed by an upright cylindrical drum on four columns – this echoes the cylindrical vaults of the building. On the second floor Isozaki has included the by now mandatory Marilyn Monroe wall beside the central staircase. The triangular motif of the central skylight is repeated in the inverted light and air distribution element suspended beneath one of the barrel vaults. 'Reduplication' is an important principle in Isozaki's second manner. In the Centre this is expressed by the repetition of identical heavily framed square

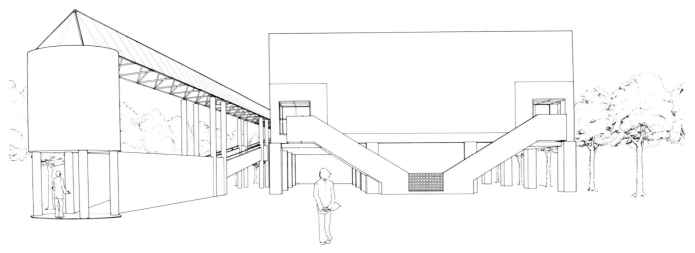

74 **Oita Audio-Visual Centre, 1978**
Perspective

windows along the side elevation.

The section through the Centre's vault is related to Louis Kahn's Kimbell Art Museum, 1966–72. In his museum Kahn opposed the curve of the barrel vault by two convex reflectors suspended in an inverted 'V'; these are not unlike Isozaki's triangular section which is a closed form and merely contrasts with the vault.

The occurrence of barrel vaults in Kahn's work in the late 1960s is noteworthy on several counts: first, it predates Isozaki's development of the vault motif in his second manner, and second, Kahn's arrangement of his vaults is inspired by Roman classical motifs, and therefore, differs substantially from Isozaki's treatment. There are similarities, notably the exposure of the vault section. However, Kahn avoids any deformation or displacement of the vault, preferring instead to repeat identical vault elements in series. Moreover, Kahn amplified the Beaux-Arts practice of putting buildings together from a number of separate pieces, each one discreet in a hierarchical order. And while Isozaki may appear to do something similar, he diverges from Kahn's method to the extent that he contrasts the geometry of the pieces in an assembly of independent, equal elements. Isozaki's method is demonstrably anti-classical and for this reason, can be seen as fundamentally different from Kahn's classicism.

By its retention of the fluid articulation of the barrel vault of the earlier schemes the Japan-Europe Cultural Centre is something of an exception when compared with other schemes from 1978 whose forms result from the intersection, rather than deformation, of the vault elements. The Nippo-European Centre resembles the Fujimi Clubhouse in several respects; its vault is a variation of the Fujimi pattern but has been modified by separating the doubled-back vault to include a broad court, it also has an entrance that is identical to the Fujimi *porte cochère*. Several new elements have been introduced, thus, a rectangular block is used to complete one side of the main court and a short length of vault added outside the court and connected to the main vault by a higher roof deck. The interior of the rectangular block already

referred to is eroded exposing a wavy edged opening between the roof and the structural frame which is exposed to the court. Quadrant shaped pavilions are disposed symmetrically on either side of the garden axis through the centre court so that their convex curved walls oppose the corners of the barrel vault. The garden axis is terminated by an open framework of five cubes across the open end of the court. The vault of the Nippo-European Centre defines the channel of movement acting as an exhibition display zone and at the same time linking administrative areas with the lecture room.

In several other of his schemes in 1978 Isozaki structured his vault forms by intersecting separate vault elements at right-angles to create 'T' junctions. This procedure eliminated the flowing curvilinear form of the earlier schemes. Consequently, whereas his earlier designs appeared to have been made from a single length or lengths of malleable pipe, these later designs give the impression of having been assembled from individual lengths of vault connected abruptly by 'T' pieces. The development of these forms can be traced from a single short length of vault on its own, to two identical vaults in tandem; these are succeeded by a single T-branch and more complex arrangements of up to three such T-branches. The project for A Women's College is based on two quadrangular vaults on either side and opening onto the central axis, a further narrow court has been added to the outer side of one of the quadrangular vaults. Once again, one is reminded by Isozaki's systematic exploration of pattern, of Ledoux's series of designs for *Barrière* and houses.

The design for A Women's College, 1978, is an experiment in the assembly of typological components to make a heterogeneous group form. It is a curious mixture of the ideal Renaissance piazza and Stirling's Schinkelesque interpretation of the Neo-Classical. Some of the typological components of the College – the theatre type from the Oita Medical Hall Annex, the cubic

framework over the dining hall, and the barrel vaulted dormitories – are taken
from Isozaki's original form stock, but others, notably the stepped octagonal
lecture hall, are new additions.

It is apparent from a comparison with his earlier work that Isozaki has
progressively isolated a series of form types, and that over a period of time he
has developed a method of composition based upon these standard forms. In
doing so, Isozaki created a serene balanced urban image, a Utopian world of
pure forms far removed from the conflicts and ambiguity of real experience,
by returning to elementary geometrical forms assembled additively and
arranged in a symmetrical manner. The unreality of this ideal architecture of
pure form is as distant from the chaotic confusion and dynamism of Tokyo
today, as the life of its women students is sheltered from the world at large.

The Hayashi Residence is the most pervasively Mannerist of Isozaki's
designs, for it invokes an impressive array of Mannerist conceits. These range
from the tendency to spatial depth and spatial incoherence, and include,
moreover, such things as Formalism alienated from reality, artificiality; reality
undermined by illusionism, spatial ambiguity, and isolation of the Residence
from its environment. The length of the entry axis, in the front vault which
precedes the cross vault, has been deliberately exaggerated, but before it can
connect with the cross vault it is interrupted by a panel of glass block above
the main stair and is broken into two fragments. Of the numerous vaulted
residences designed by Isozaki before 1978 the Hayashi House is the most
ambitious in terms of its scale and complexity of form. In plan the vault
resembles a two pronged tuning fork. The intersection of the four vault

elements produces precise arrises. The curved lines of intersection of the semi-circular vault under-surfaces are multiplied, and the coherence of the interior space is obscured by the use of mirrors, transparent screens, and by painting them white to give them a dimensionless quality.

Entry to the house is gained by means of a vaulted portico which introduces a ramp with the main stair leading off on one side. The main living and sleeping spaces on the first and second floors are located within the vaulted block reached at the end of the ramp. The main stair is lit by a panel of glass block which interrupts the long entry vault. The living, dining, and kitchen areas are situated on the first floor and an opening is left above the living room to relate its space to the vault above. The main bedroom is reached through a closeted dressing room, which when darkened, reflects the

77 **Hayashi House, 1978**
Illusion is heightened by the use of mirrors to reflect the adjacent glass block vault in the darkened dressing room

151

109

glass block vault on the mirror-faced doors of the closets on either side of the hall. The main bedroom is positioned on the central axis between the two short vaults and this results in a highly complex intersection of vaulted spaces on either side.

152

Low contrasting walls isolate the vaults from the floor, and glass screens between these walls and the soffit of the vaults produce multiple images of the vaults; the effect of this is to blur the boundary between reality and illusion. In addition, the transparent screens assure the visual continuity of the vaults while allowing a degree of physical subdivision of the interior without interrupting the central axis. Square shapes reverberate throughout the house: in the window openings below the double barrel vaults, in the cubic gatehouse, and in the subdivision of the glass walls. And once more Marilyn Monroe's ubiquitous profile defines the boundary of the entry terraces.

Classicism: the Search for a New Theme

The new element of classicism in Isozaki's recent architecture – something shared by Fumihiko Maki in his library for Keio University, Tokyo – raises the prospect that his work is entering a new phase. If so, the new classicism of the Tsukuba Civic Centre is hardly a transient phenomenon, but rather it is the harbinger of something much more lasting and therefore important. The emergence of classicism at this point in Isozaki's architecture should not come as a surprise since the second manner contained a strong Neo-Classical bias, therefore it was natural and, in a sense, to be expected, for this to lead in time to a new classicism.

157

The N.E.G. Employees Building was developed to provide recreation and dining facilities for the employees of the Ootsu factory of Nippon Electric Glass Co., Ltd. It consists of two principal elements: a simple steel cage encased in glass block and panels of crystallised glass with exposed diagonal bracing ties to resist wind loads and earthquakes, around which Isozaki wrapped a curved screen behind which is the guest dining room. The effect of this is to confront and partially obscure the pure glass block by a thin striped wall of hollow Asbestolux panels and glass blocks. Neo-Classicism arose in the eighteenth century as a reaction to the baroque. It is as though, seemingly, Isozaki recognised this stylistic dichotomy by juxtaposing two distinct

155

systems of form: the curved screen wall enfolding and contrasting with the austere steel and glass main block – a confrontation of opposites in effect.

Much could, and should perhaps, be said, concerning the introduction of permanent polychrome for the facade. Its most immediate antecedents are Robert Stern's Westchester Residence, Armonk, 1974–6, and Minoru Takeyama's Ni-Ban-Kahn building with its extroverted deployment of large scale graphic devices. The development of polychrome, subsequent to Italian Romanesque, is credited to the English architect William Butterfield whose All Saints Church, 1850–9, employed red and black banded brickwork for the first time in London.

156

The permanent polychrome treatment of brown and yellow banded Asbestolux panels is carried inside into the guest dining room where a grey and white scheme of horizontal bands complements the freely curved glass block screen. The N.E.G. Employees Facility is a hybrid work which continues in a simplified way themes from Isozaki's earlier second manner. However, the Tsukuba Civic Centre breaks new ground. One is tempted even to compare the main block with Fumihiko Maki's Central Building of the Faculty of Physical Education for Tsukuba University, 1974.

Isozaki is acutely sensitive to new currents among the *avant-garde* of America and Europe. It is debatable whether such a close, even incestuous, exchange of ideas between a well defined international architectural elite can be carried on for very long before the limited nature of the exchange leads to sterility and an alienation from reality. Thus the *trompe-l'oeil* capitals painted on the ceiling of the dining room and the overstated black cylindrical bases – a caricature of the classical order – confirm the influence of Michael Graves. Graves's highly mannered interpretation of classicism reduces the classical elements to their most primitive components while simultaneously exaggerating and distorting their forms for effect.

The shift in Isozaki's architecture from the second manner to a distorted kind of classicism is especially evident in his scheme for the Civic Centre for Tsukuba Academic New Town. Tsukuba is located some 60 km north-east of Tokyo and was planned as a centre for various national research institutes, laboratories and Tsukuba University. However, the absence of amenities, a civic centre and the attractions of city life severely limited the appeal of the city and its growth has been slow. Isozaki set out to give the fledgeling city a central 'place' in order to assist its new inhabitants to orientate themselves in the world and thereby enable them to experience a sense of dwelling. The sunken forum establishes an *axis-mundi* for the new city so necessary if people *158* are to feel orientated in the world.

In his Civic Centre, planned for completion in 1982, Isozaki enclosed an inverted Surrealistic version of Michelangelo's Piazza of the Campidoglio on two sides by a concert hall, hotel and shops. The fenestration of the buildings is a mixture of Ledoux and Michael Graves with occasional dashes of Aldo Rossi. Thus, the porch adjoining the concert hall and the plaza entrance of the *160* hotel are inspired by elevations from Ledoux's Royal Saltworks at Arc-et-Senans. Ledoux's bandaged column shafts are repeated in the entrances of the hotel and the gateway to the concert hall. The debasement of the column shafts is meant to convey a picture of the visible disintegration of the columnar order in the face of an onslaught by an active wall.

The completeness of the sunken forum is violated by a cascade which *159* gushes forth from beneath the open air theatre and finds it way down a series of irregular ledges to a circular pool in the centre. This is yet another depiction of the antagonism of nature and man's works with nature corrupting the perfection of man's creation and moving to its very heart-centre. A similar theme is echoed in the hotel and concert hall facades where a rusticated base storey of cast-on-site artificial stone is opposed by silver ceramic tile and aluminium panel facings on the upper storeys.

The Tsukuba Civic Centre is the strongest essay in Neo-Classicism from Isozaki to date. Nevertheless, Isozaki has chosen a recognisably Mannerist interpretation of Ledoux for he is not content to transcribe Ledoux's motifs directly, instead he twists and distorts the forms. If the content of the forms is

Neo-Classical it is also true that their organisation continues to be thoroughly Mannerist.

161   The Tegel Harbour Competition scheme of October 1980, is extremely sophisticated inasmuch as it seeks to draw out relationships with the Schloss Tegel of 1822 and hence with the architectural milieu of Karl Friedrich Schinkel, and is based on a quite complex series of interior relationships between individuated type-functions. The scheme is a further demonstration of Isozaki's method which he has described as a 'metaphor making machine' and his current formal Neo-Classical orientation. The competition was a fortunate event, in so far as it supplied Isozaki with a ready-made opportunity to extend these ideas in an urban context which required a formal response in keeping with Schinkel.

162   The architectural realization of the programme for three different functions – a cultural and recreational centre and housing – was satisfied with two juxtaposed U-shaped blocks which confront one another across Medebacher Strasse. Their symmetry has been emphasised further by two pairs of cubes.

The poetic imagery chosen by Isozaki, that of a giant ship stranded on land – something like Hans Hollein's aircraft carrier collage – and the wave-shaped suspended roof of the gymnasium is reminiscent of the Kitakyushu Municipal Exhibition Hall. Even the curved end wall of the Kitakyushu restaurant has been repeated at the east and west ends of the U-shaped blocks. Furthermore, as in the Kitakyushu building, Isozaki has returned to a tension roof structure – a simply suspended 4·5 mm corten steel (a special type of steel with a hard protective coating which prevents further oxidisation) sheet roof in this instance – to evoke maritime associations. Isozaki's poetic use of imagery parallels Utzon's evocation of flapping gulls' wings, sail shapes, and wave motion for the Sydney Opera House in 1956 to relate his building to the surrounding harbour, but whereas Utzon is a romantic, Isozaki's method of composing and relating the parts within the building form is fundamentally Mannerist, even where, as here, his forms are outwardly Neo-Classical.

The Tegel Harbour Competition was an important one for Isozaki as can be gauged from the meticulous presentation of the scheme which won him third

163   place after Charles Moore and Ralph Erskine. The application of such contrastive concepts as urban/rural, geometric/organic, artificial/natural and hard/soft, in combination with the quotation and reconstruction of features from Schinkel's Schloss Tegel, is carried through with great mastery. Isozaki chose to juxtapose and interpenetrate the individual type-forms to produce a Mannerist assemblage. The semi-circular central area adjoining the north-south orientated plaza is an adaptation of the earlier Kamioka Town Hall motif. It is connected to the library and music school by a sensual Marilyn Monroe shaped foyer; this profile is echoed in the restaurant and garden. The entire Tegel Harbour scheme is an interlocking assembly of complete, self-sufficient elements which have been so juxtaposed, contrasted, and interconnected as to produce a diverse, although none the less, fragmented heterogeneous form. The influence of Leon Krier is evident in the treatment of the housing block on the west and in the expression of the gateways.

Isozaki's scheme, as *Architectural Design* rightly observed, deserved a more favourable response from the Berlin politicians and the Tegel residents than it was accorded, since 'His harmonious marriage of Japanese and Schinkelesque elements produced a significant architectural statement that in many respects deserved to be realised'.*

In the Tsukuba Civic Centre and the Tegel Harbour Competition scheme Isozaki employed a type of Surrealistic 'collage' which was latent in the Modern Movement. In a Surrealistic 'collage' the elements, some which have been derived from Ledoux, are reconstituted to make a fragmented heterogeneous assemblage. Both the Tsukuba Civic Centre and the Tegel Harbour Scheme should be seen in the context of a revival of Neo-Classical sources in the late 1970s symptomatic of a deeper aesthetic reorientation and return to Formalism.

Architecture in Transition

It is rare for history to witness an uninterrupted succession of periods of high creative achievement, such golden moments whether in the life of a nation or an individual are more usually separated by intervening periods of consolidation, simple expansion, or even regression. In the 1960s and 1970s architects sought to distance their work from that great phase in the early part of the twentieth century referred to as the Modern Movement which has overshadowed so much that followed. Consequently, the 1960s and 1970s became a time of struggle and protest against Modern architecture; decades in which architects sought new ways of thinking about and doing architecture, ways which, wherever possible, were the antithesis of Modernism.

It needs to be asked what has been Isozaki's particular contribution during this phase of architectural reaction? The answer to this question, I would suggest, lies in his special ability to define the crisis of Modernism and to create out of this situation a number of highly successful and utterly convincing buildings which treat architecture as a kind of concrete poetry, for Isozaki brings to architecture a unique poetic perception and sensibility. His architecture gives special significance to other architecture, and to the work of his contemporaries; it is inspired by architecture itself no less. Because Isozaki's method parallels Mannerism in so many respects his architecture speaks of nothing so eloquently as other architecture.

Within Japan Isozaki chose for himself the role of the leading exponent and interpreter of the new anti-Modern ideas, which in addition to revoking a number of the taboos connected with Modernism, such as eclecticism, applied decoration, and the classical orders and mouldings, led to the rise of a new high formalism and monumentality in architecture. Such things as the expression of the building as a symbolic object, the recovery of the facade as an articulate form, the creation of a new monumentality and the exploitation of historic memory with the freeing of inhibitions towards the past has given a new dimension of freedom and liberation from the dogmas of Modernism.

Isozaki's architecture accurately reflects the changes in taste of a quite small international intellectual elite, so much so, that his architecture is inexplicable

*Architectural Design Supplement, November, 1980.

if it is considered in isolation from developments in architectural thinking which have occurred in New York, London, and Vienna. There is a real danger that this somewhat restrictive and exclusive *avante-garde* feeding off itself will in time become incestuous and sterile, alienated from the real world.

World architecture has, and still is, undergoing deep change for without doubt the 1970s was a period of transition, but as yet no single principle or set of ideas has come to dominate the centre stage to give architecture a degree of coherence implied by the term Post Modern architecture. Under the circumstances Mannerism, or rather a kind of quasi-Mannerism, provided an aesthetic viewpoint which to a considerable extent was able to give significance to the fragmentation, diversity, and conflicting reality which typifies our world today. Prior to the Hayashi House Isozaki's work represented a self-conscious and highly artificial exercise of Mannerist formulae, but with this building he moved towards a more natural and fluent Mannerist idiom. By 1978 Isozaki had perfected his style and made it his own. This second manner drew on a wide range of historical materials and combined them in a loose Surrealistic 'Collage'. In his more recent works a popular Manneristic idiom has emerged which is as cheap and sensible as it is stylish. In his struggle for style Isozaki made style itself the goal of his architecture, with the result that style has become an end in itself, replacing the preceding Rationalism of Modern architecture.

Works 1960—1980

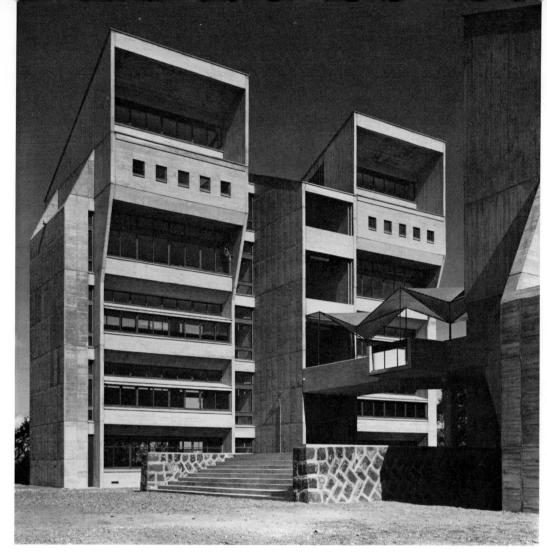

78–79 Iwata Girls' High School, Iwata-cho, Oita, 1963–4
Frontal view of classroom towers

79 Site plan

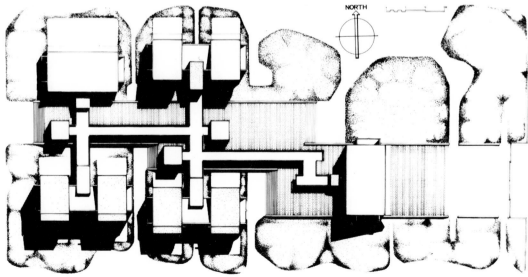

NORTH

80

80–2   Oita Prefectural Library, Niage-cho, Oita, 1962–6

80   View of raised entry, the ramp leads to the entrance hall

81   The reading room is spanned by two sizes of inverted U-section concrete beams

82   Oblique projection of the underside of the roof. The diagram exposes the simple trabeated arrangement of the enlarged roof beams

81

82

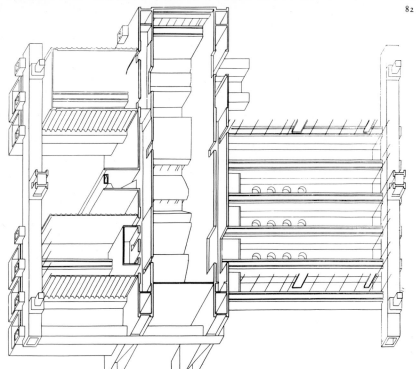

119

83

84

85

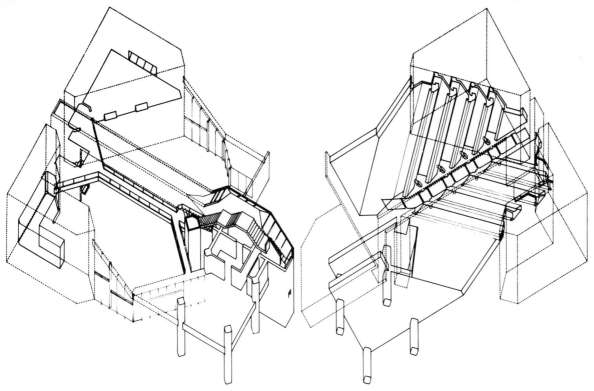

86–88 Daimyo branch, Fukuoka Mutual Bank, 1967–70

86 Upper volume over the business room. Reflected daylight from a concealed skylight gives the space a vertical emphasis

87 Section

88 Lobby. The semi-circular glass screens contrast with the 45° geometry of the main space

86

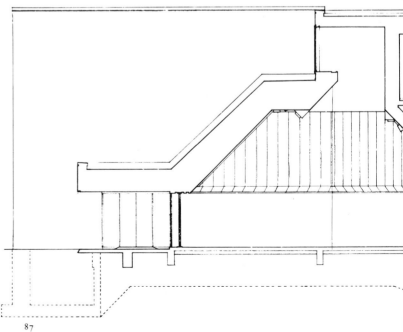

87

89–94 Headquarters, Fukuoka Mutual Bank, Fukuoka, 1968–71

89 Projecting outrigger beam. The outsize beams are relics from the megaskeletal manner which has been overtaken by a new Neo-Classical expression

90 Reception room in the executive suite

91 Entry hall. The simple cube shape of the space harks back to the Renaissance revival of neo-Platonic geometry

89

90

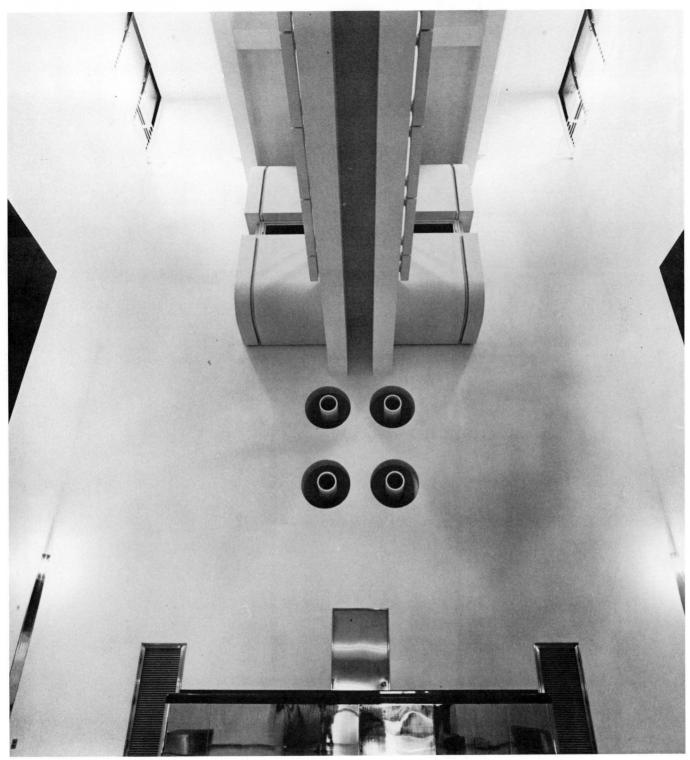

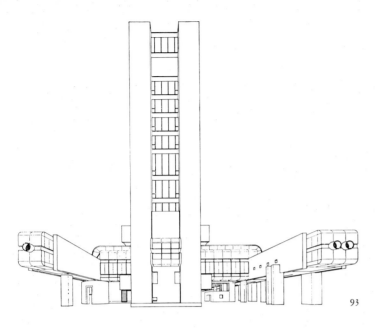

93 End view. The elevated outrigger beams are tied in to the main office structure by exposed beams

94 Plans (*a*) and section (*b*): roof 6th floor (*c*), 4th floor (*d*), first floor (*e*)

Key: 1. conference room; 2. lobby; 3. business room; 4. parking; 5. library; 6. office; 7. reception room; 8. void; 9. president's room; 10. chairman's room; 11. executive room; 12. secretary's room

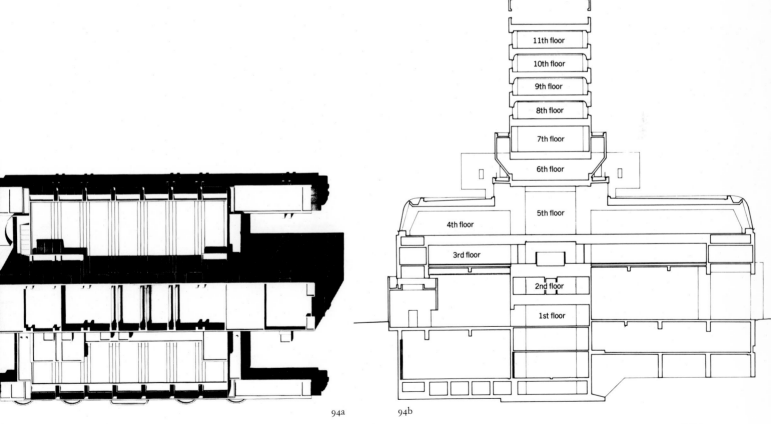

94a   94b

11th floor
10th floor
9th floor
8th floor
7th floor
6th floor
5th floor
4th floor
3rd floor
2nd floor
1st floor

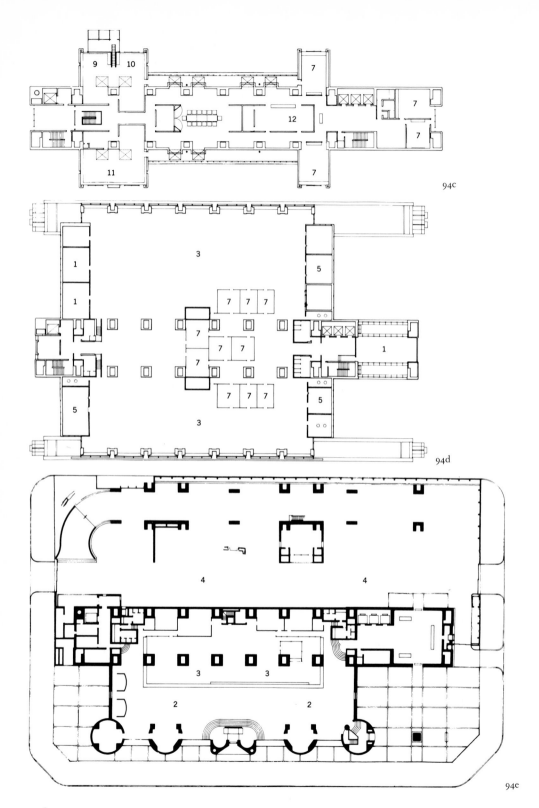

94c

94d

94e

95–99 **Kitakyusha City Museum of Art, Kitakyushu, 1972–4**

95 The raised cast-aluminium-clad beams housing the galleries are supported by exposed concrete platforms on a ridge overlooking Kitakyushu

97

98

96　Entrance hall. All the surfaces are shiny. Italian marble is used on the floor and walls, cast-aluminium for the great beams

97　View from the bridge, second floor, overlooking the entrance hall

98　Skylight corridor access to restaurant, second floor

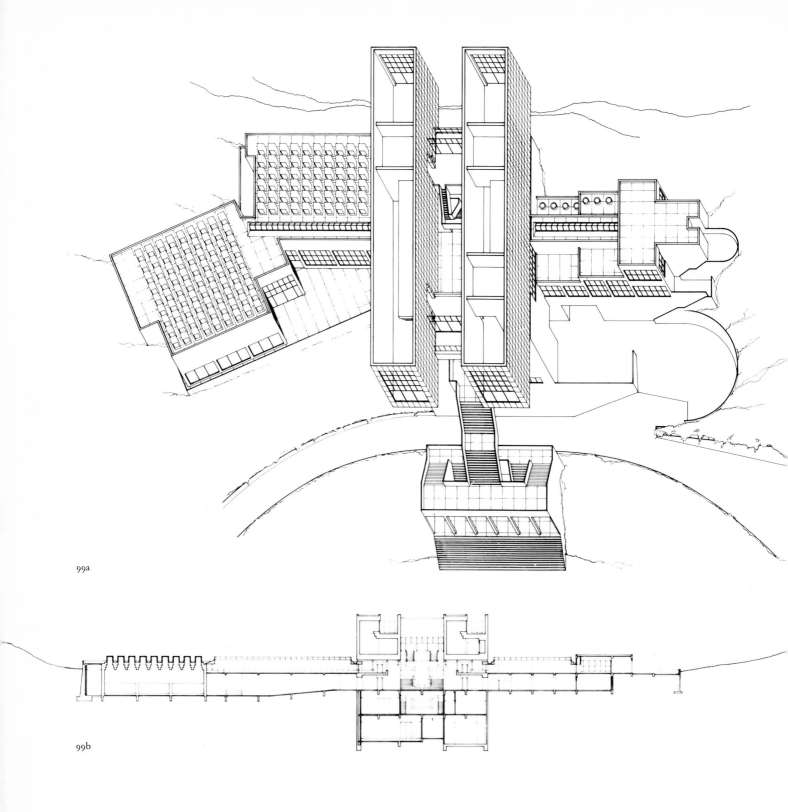

99a

99b

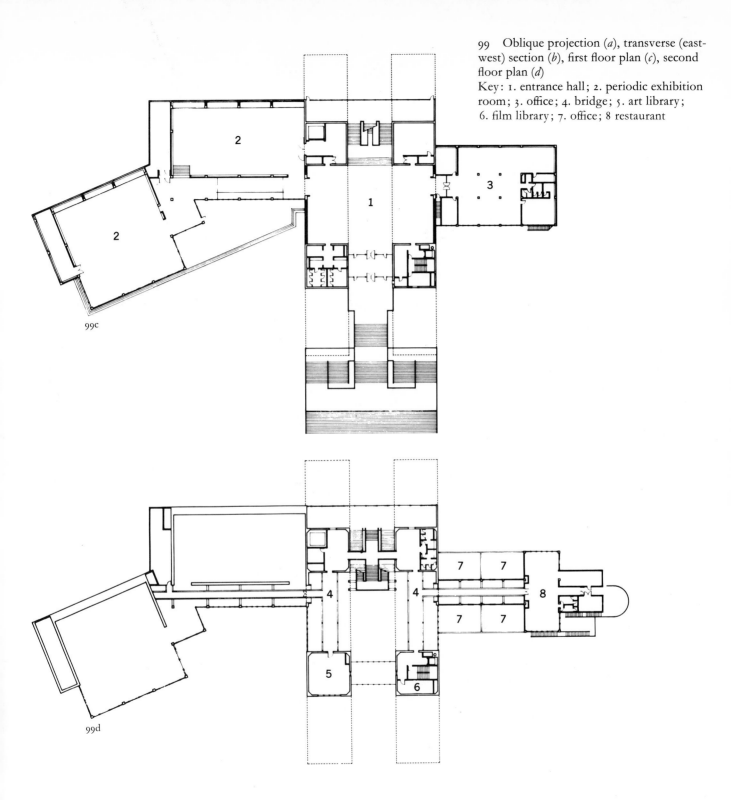

99 Oblique projection (*a*), transverse (east-west) section (*b*), first floor plan (*c*), second floor plan (*d*)
Key: 1. entrance hall; 2. periodic exhibition room; 3. office; 4. bridge; 5. art library; 6. film library; 7. office; 8 restaurant

99c

99d

100

101

134

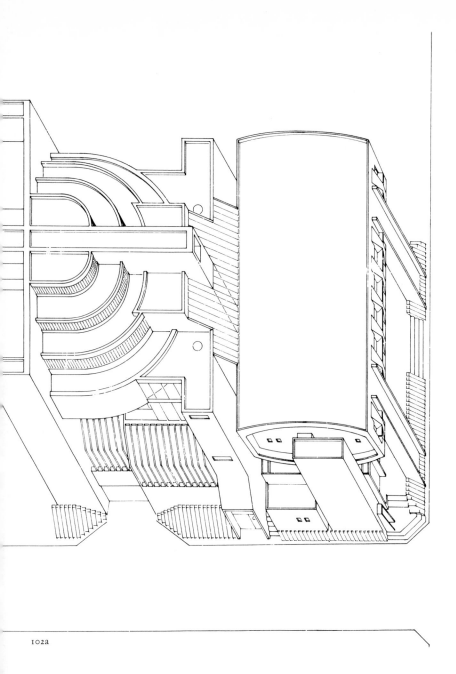
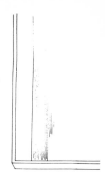

102a

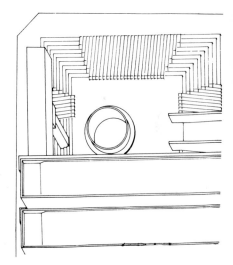

100–102 Oita Medical Hall Annex, Niage-cho, Oita, 1970–2

100 Stepped roof of the main conference room, third floor

101 Bridge connection, second floor

102 Oblique projection (*a*), third floor plan (*b*), second floor plan (*c*)
Key: 4. void; 5. conference room; 6. chairman's room; 7. library; 8. main conference room; 9. auditorium of third floor

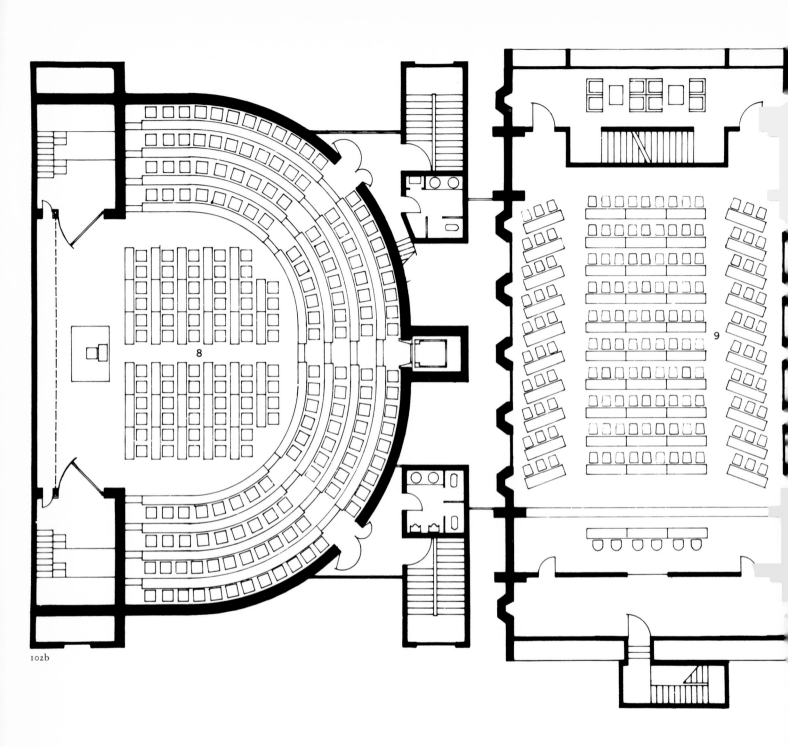

102b

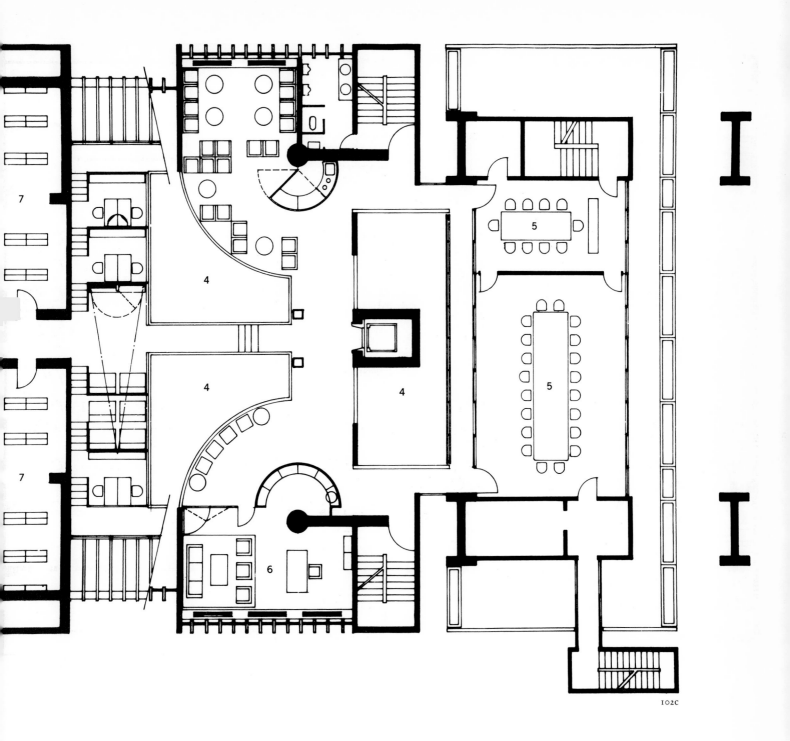

102C

103

103 **Nakayama House and Clinic, Oita,**
1964
View at night

138

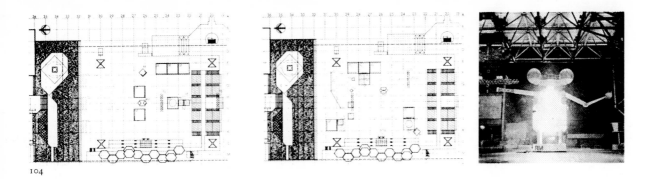

104

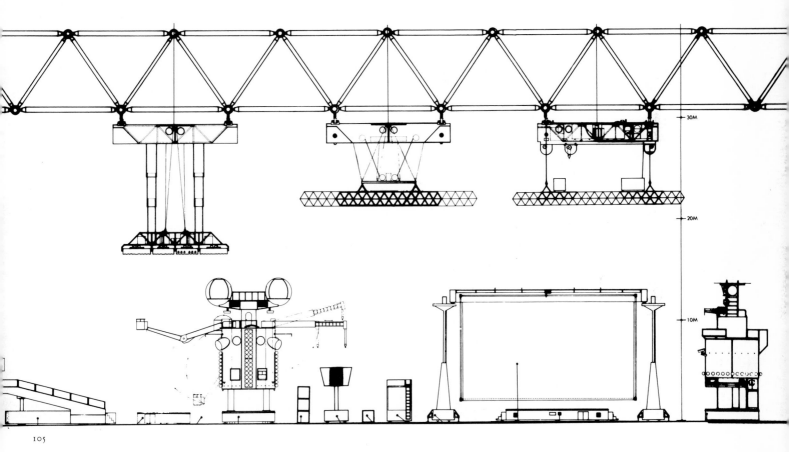

105

104 Festival Plaza, Expo '70, Suita, Osaka, 1967–70

105 Section, plans

139

106 View of street facade and parking

107 Office

108 First floor plan
Key: 1. business room; 2. lobby;
3. parking; 4. safe; 5. garage; 6. electricity room

107

108

141

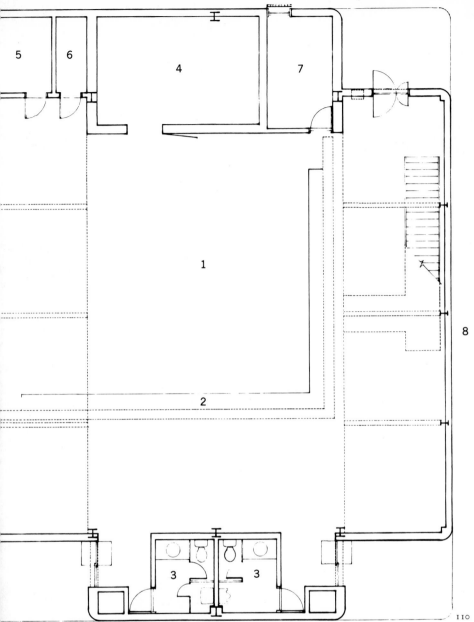

109–110 **Roppomatsu branch, Fukuoka Mutual Bank, Chuo-ku, Fukuoka, 1971–2**

109 Interior, business room

110 First floor plan
Key: 1. office; 2. counter; 3. toilet; 4. safe;
5. kitchen; 6. storage; 7. suite; 8. parking

110

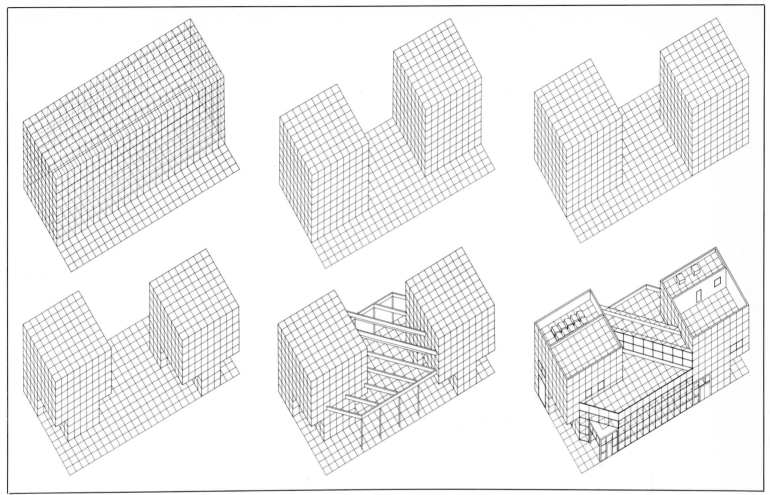

111–112   Saga branch, Fukuoka Mutual Bank, 1972–3

111   View of business room

112   Development of form from two spaced cubes (*a*) and roof plan (*b*)

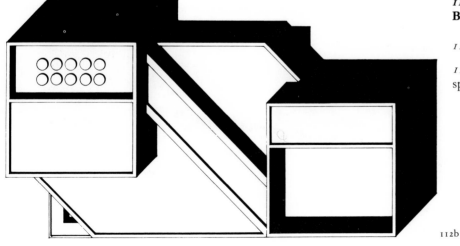

112b

113

114

115

116 Exhibition wing for traditional
Japanese art seen from the entrance lobby

117 South elevation of entry hall with
second floor restaurant framed within the
large cube of the main structure

149

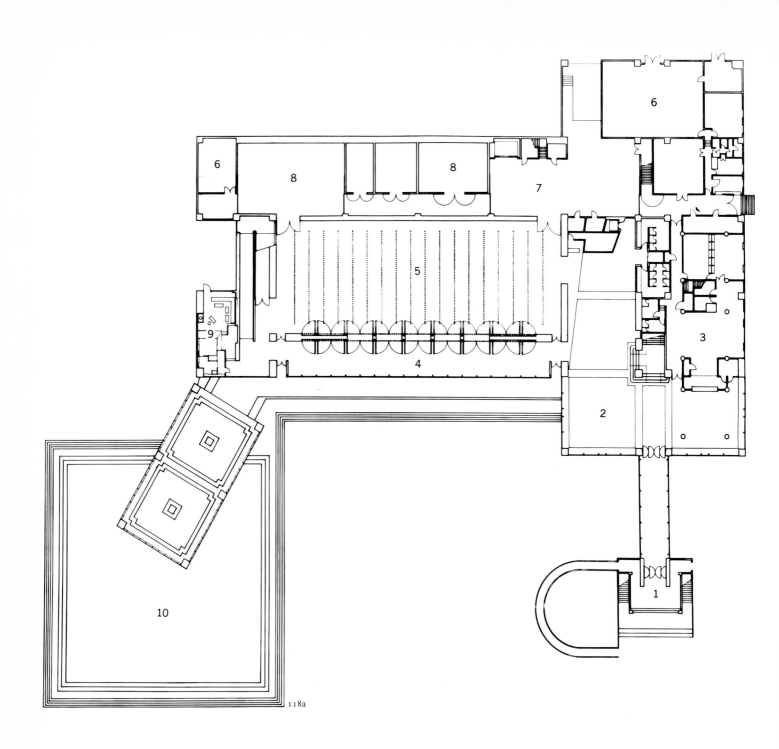

118a

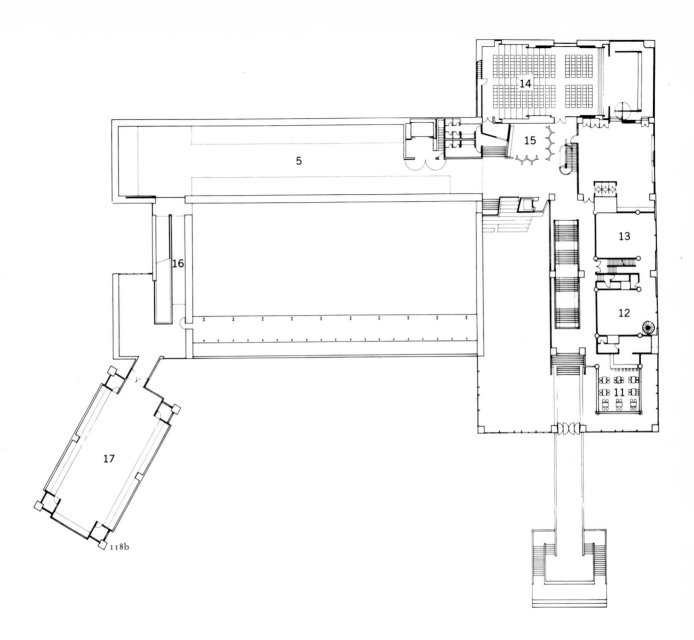

118b

118 First floor plan (*a*), second floor
plan (*b*)
Key: 1. entrance; 2. lobby; 3. office;
4. gallery; 5. exhibition room;
6. machinery; 7. unloading room;
8. storage; 9. tea house; 10. pond;
11. restaurant; 12. study; 13. library;
14. lecture room; 15. browsing; 16. ramp;
17. exhibition hall for Japanese art
(Yamatane Memorial Hall)

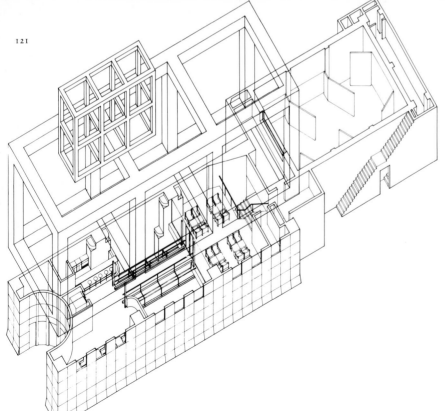

121

119–121 Shukosha Building, Fukuoka, 1974–5

119 Clients' room on the fifth floor seen from the bridge in front of the elevator

120 View of second floor bridge overlooking the first floor gallery

121 Axonometric. The conceptual structure for the architectural form is based on a composition of six large cubes surmounted by six small cubes

122–125 **West Japan General Exhibition Centre, Kitakyushu, 1975–7**

122 Night view, east facade

123   Mast and cable structure south façade

124   View from south east

123

124

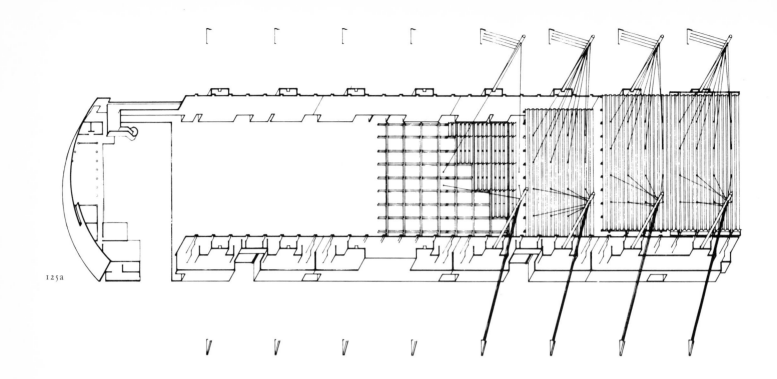

125a

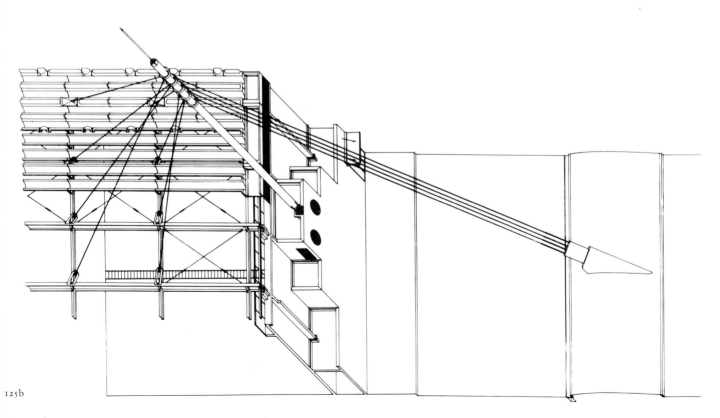

125b

156

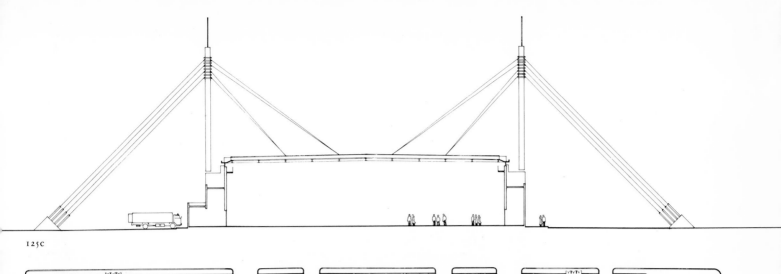

125c

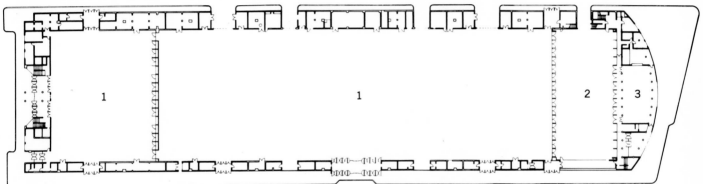

125d

125 Oblique projection of exhibition hall
roof deck and mast and cable stay
arrangement (*a*), detail of structural system
(*b*), section (*c*), and plan (*d*)
Key: 1. exhibition hall; 2. court;
3. restaurant

157

126–131 Kamioka Town Hall, Kamioka, 1976–8

126 General view from north

127 East elevation, main entry

128 Semi-circular brick plaza, in front of the main foyer

158

126

127
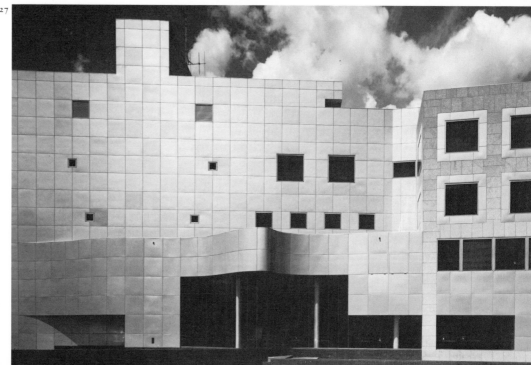

129   Two storey public hall assumes the
form of a circular temple partly buried
within the west façade

130   Council chamber

131   Plans: first floor (*a*), 4th floor (*b*) and
fifth floor (*c*)
Key: 1. plaza; 2. lobby; 3. public hall;
4. open office area; 5. council chamber

160

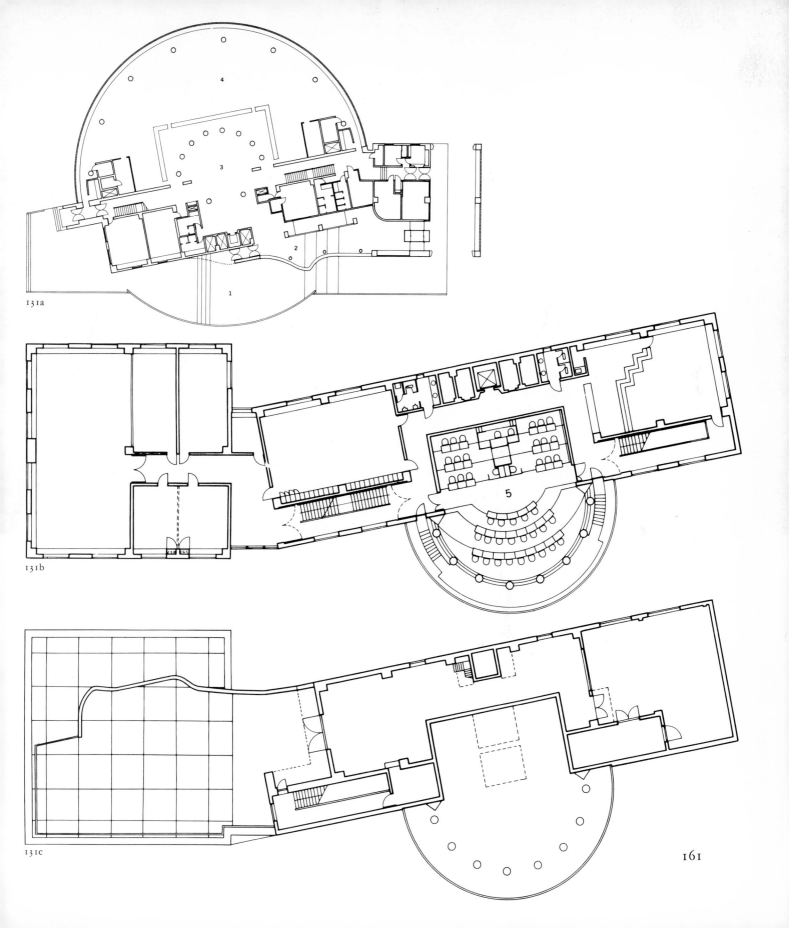

131a

131b

131c

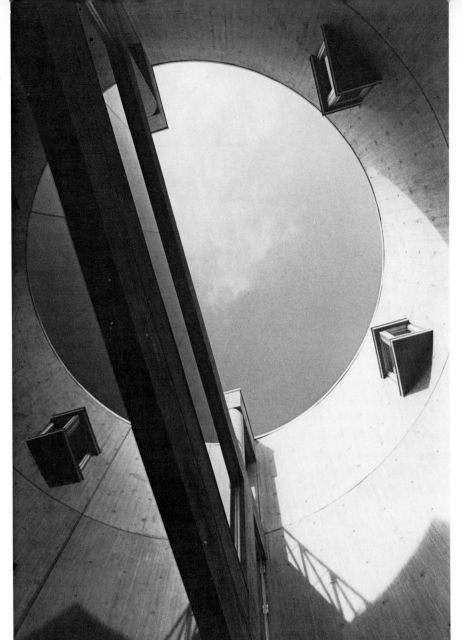

132

133

134 **Computer Aided City, 1970–72**
View of model

135–139 Yano House, Kawasaki (on the outskirts of Tokyo), 1975

135 General view. The flat-roof building on the right is an occultist's office, completed in 1974

136 Study seen from the bedroom

137 Living room seen from the entrance hall

138 East side of the living room

135

136

139 Axonometric (*a*), north-south section
(*b* left), east-west section (*b* right), first floor
plan (*c* top), second floor plan (*c* middle),
and roof plan (*c* bottom)
Key: 1. living room; 2. dining alcove;
3. kitchen; 4. pantry; 5. terrace; 6. guest
room; 7. entrance; 8. boiler room; 9. bath
room; 10. study; 11. bedroom

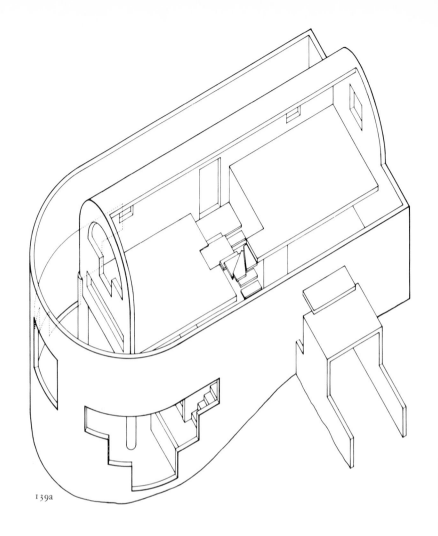

139a

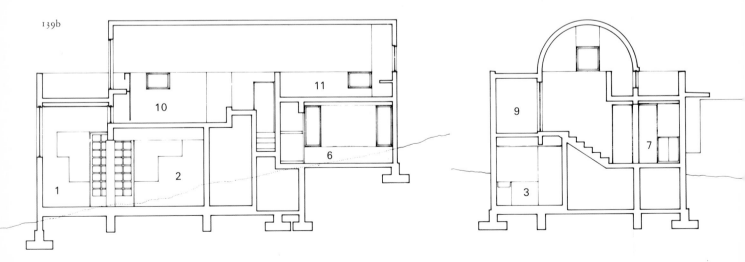

139b

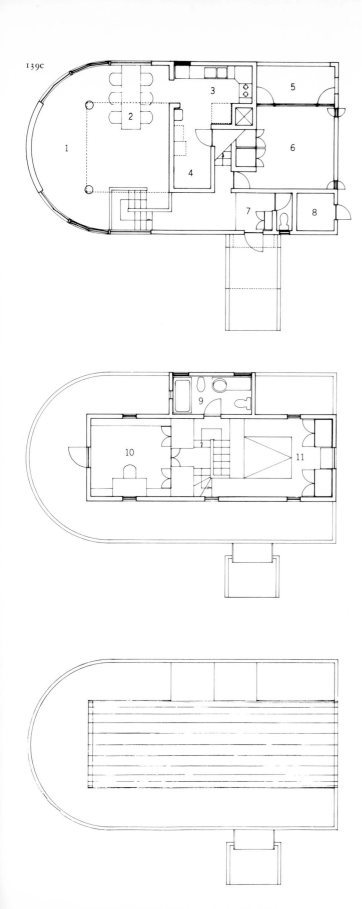

139c

140–146 Fujimi Country Clubhouse, near Oita, 1972–4

140 General view with *porte-cochère* in foreground

141 Vault covered entry reminiscent of Palladio's Villa Poiana

142 Entrance foyer, on first floor

143 View of the meeting room from the dining room on second floor

141

142

143

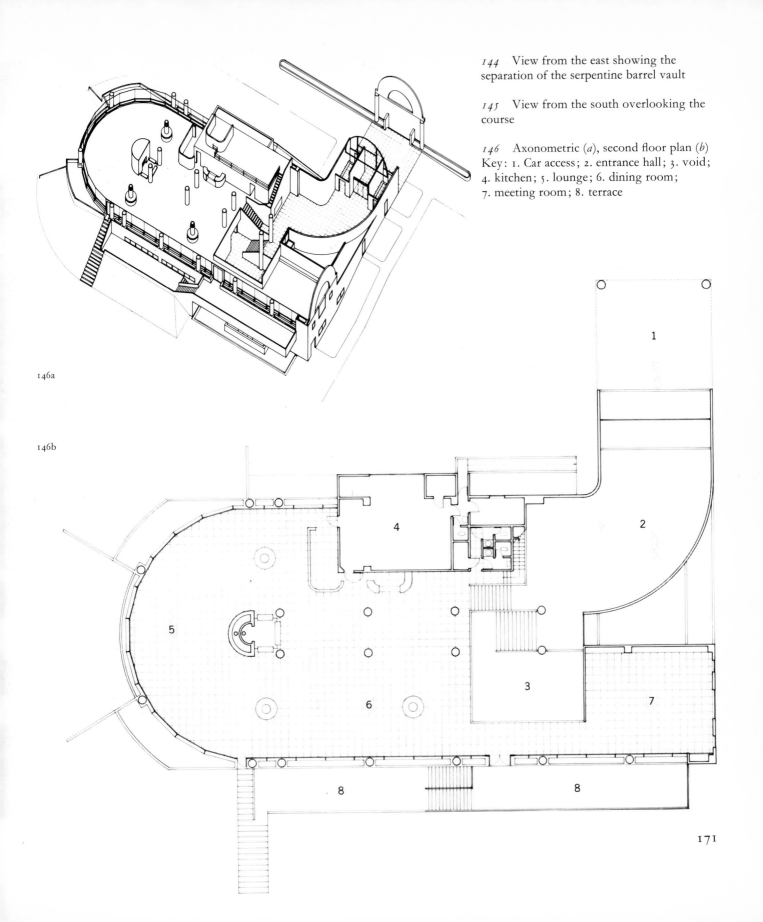

144 View from the east showing the separation of the serpentine barrel vault

145 View from the south overlooking the course

146 Axonometric (*a*), second floor plan (*b*)
Key: 1. Car access; 2. entrance hall; 3. void;
4. kitchen; 5. lounge; 6. dining room;
7. meeting room; 8. terrace

146a

146b

147

147–150   **Central Library for the City of Kyushu, Kokura-kita-cho, Kitakyushu, 1972–5**

147   View from east of the exhibition hall

148   Reference library on the second floor

149   Curved vault overlooking the first floor lobby

172

148

149

173

ЕЕ

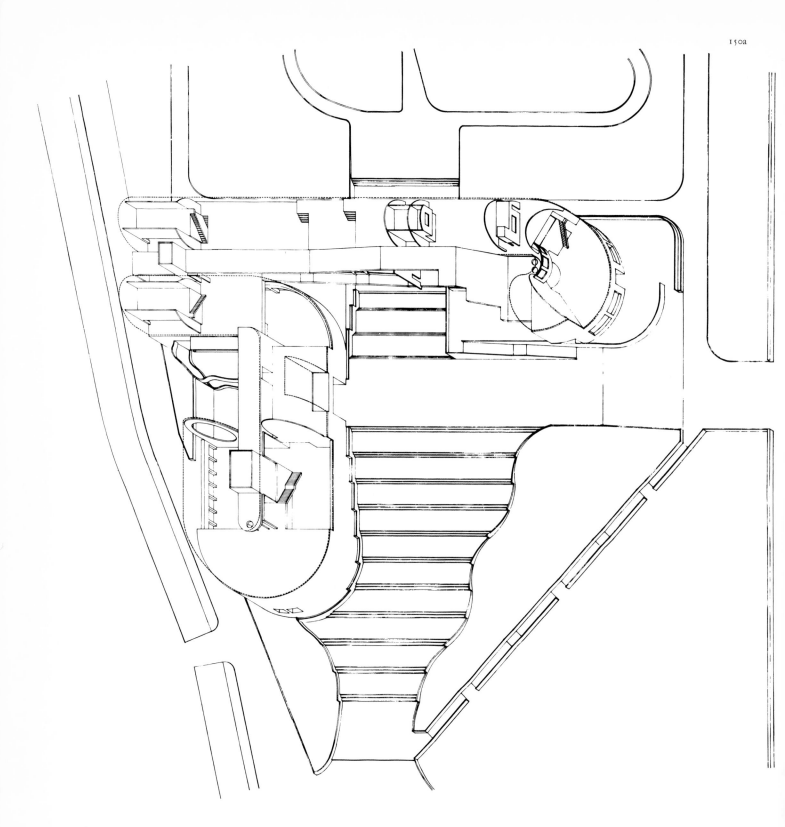

ЕЕ

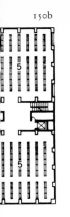

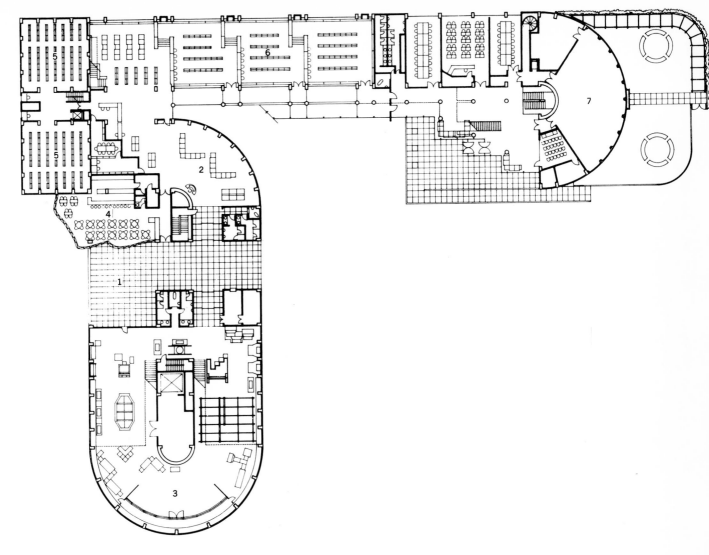

150 Axonometric (*a*), first floor plan (*b*), and second floor plan (*c*)
Key: 1. Entrance; 2. lobby; 3. exhibition hall; 4. restaurant; 5. stack room; 6. general library; 7. studio; 8. study area; 9. folk resources room; 10. void

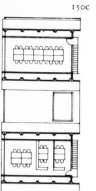

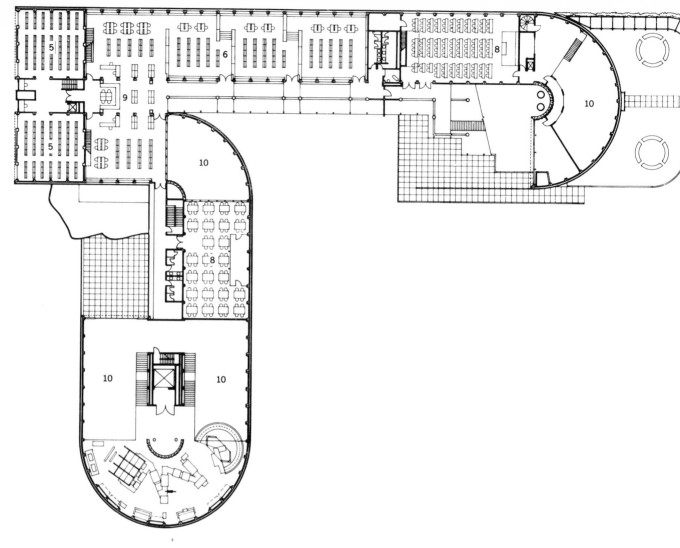

151–153 **Hayashi House, 1978**

151 Interior, two storey living room looking into conversation alcove

151

153a

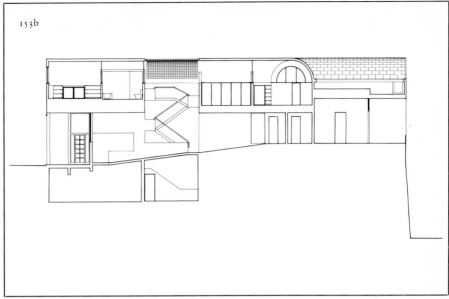

153b

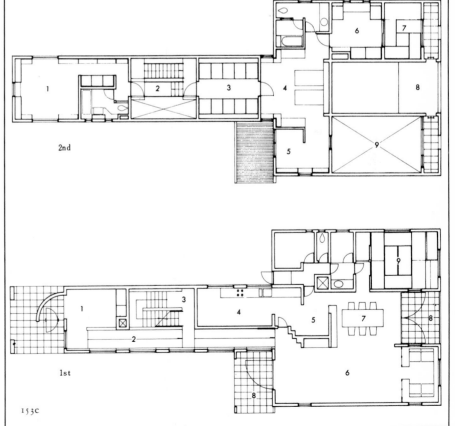

2nd

1st

153c

152 View of Japanese room from music area

153 Oblique diagram (*a*), sections (*b*), first floor plan, and second floor plan (*c*)

Key: First floor plan (below) 1. entry; 2. ramp; 3. stair; 4. kitchen; 5. alcove; 6. dining; 7. living; 8. terrace; 9. Japanese room
Second floor plan (above) 1. study; 2. stair; 3. dressing room; 4. bedroom; 5. study; 6. music area; 7. 5½ mat room; 8. roof deck; 9. void

155

**154–157   Nippon Electric Glass Co. Ltd
Employees' Service Facilities, Ootsu,
1978–1980**

154   Main façade

155   North-west corner of the guest dining
room. The fluid crystallised glass wall in
front of the dining room overlays and
obscures the main block

156   Guest dining room. The polychrome
treatment of the exterior Asbestolux
panelling has been carried inside

157   Axonometric (first scheme)

180

156

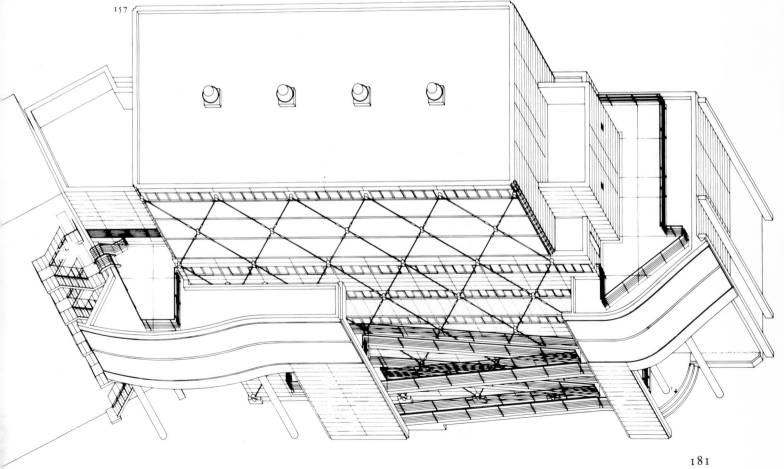

157

158–160 Tsukuba Civic Centre Project, Tsukuba Academic New Town, 1979–82

158 Bird's eye view of the sunken plaza on the axis of the city

159 The plaza is intended as a surreal

inversion of Michelangelo's piazzo of the Campidoglio

Key: 1. exhibition room; 2. foyer; 3. concert hall; 4. balcony; 5. projection room; 6. restaurant; 7. coffee shop; 8. bank; 9. lobby; 10. Japanese restaurant; 11. forum; 12. open-air theatre; 13. cascade

160 Gateway to the concert hall. Isozaki has once again revived the Mannerist conflict between the wall and the imposed classical order, and that of rustication and smooth surfaces, the former representing nature, the latter the works of man

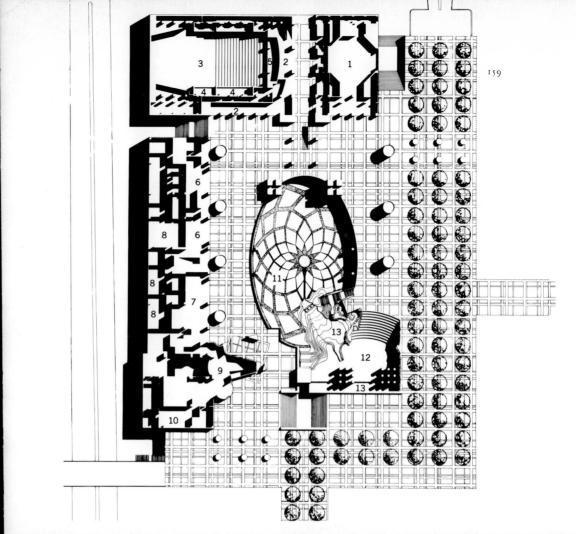

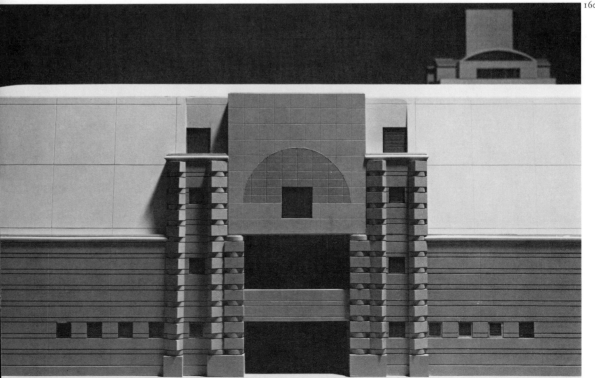

161–163 Tegel Harbour Competition Scheme, Berlin, October 1980

161 Model. Aerial view from west with Tegel Harbour in the foreground. The transposed façade from the Humboldt Mansion and the semi-circular cultural

centre enclose two sides of the plaza. The sports centre, situated behind the cultural centre is enclosed by a suspended cor-ten steel roof. To the west, the residential block faces on to a court open at one end

162 Aerial view from south. The cultural

centre and recreation centre on the right ar separated from the U-shaped residential block by Medebacher Strasse

163 Perspective from across the harbour

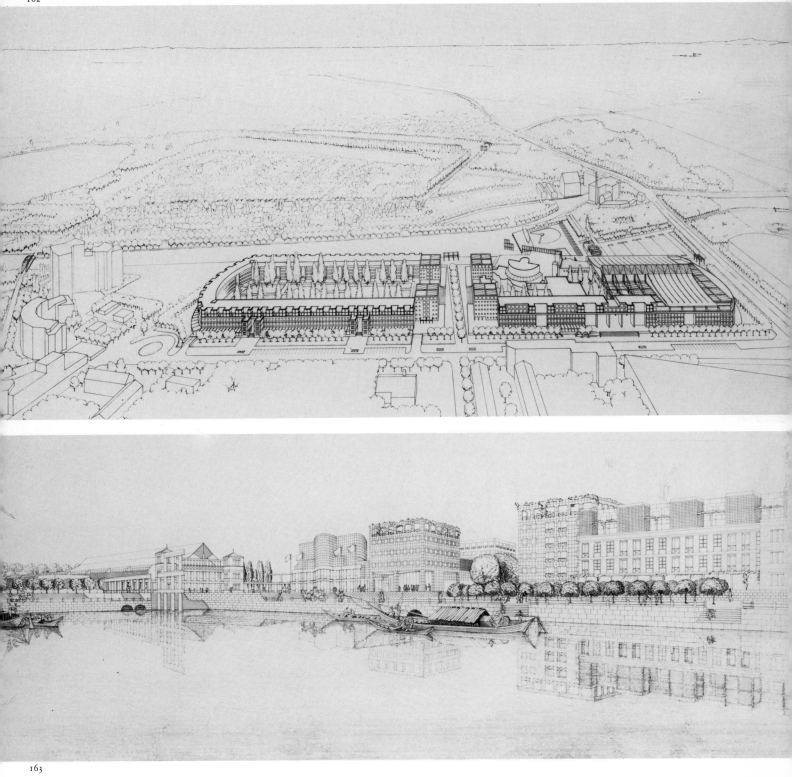

An Architecture of Quotation and Metaphor, 1978

by *Arata Isozaki*

An Architecture of Quotation and Metaphor

This essay was originally published in the *Hankenchiku-Tei Note* (Anti-architecture Note) series in the Japanese magazine *Kenchiku Bunka* **33**, 9 (September, 1978.) 33–5.
The original English translation by Hajime Yatsuka and Lynne Breslin has been revised to clarify some of the more difficult arguments presented in the text. 'An Architecture of Quotation and Metaphor' supersedes an earlier 1972 essay 'Manner is Everything' as the most up-to-date and complete statement of Isozaki's approach to architecture.

The 1960s was spent in a deliberate attack on the normative concepts of the Modern architecture, freeing us in the 1970s to concentrate on 'Architecture' itself and on the elaboration of our method. My generation has arrived at the point where Modern architecture can be justifiably relegated to the past. The theoretical writings of Pevsner, Giedion, and Banham on Modern architecture have identified the development of a technological nexus engendering a unique industrial society forged by its function as a productive system. This then has become the central theme of that architecture, creating in turn a style apart from all styles, whose content is unique. The momentum of that architecture propelled us through the 1950s but stalled by the 1960s. In my book *Kenchiku-no-kaitai* I attempted to introduce the means of deviating, transforming, and ultimately negating it.

Only now have we overcome the postulate that Modern architecture is the straightforward expression of technology, to recognise the mediating forces that have always circumscribed architecture: the formal self-referential impulse. Reyner Banham and Colin Rowe drew attention to this phenomenon, and in so doing, enabled us to see the Modern Movement for what it was, one of the many historical legacies available to us as texts. For now Modern architecture can be seen not merely as a successive development open to negotiation, but rather as a text and as such, a rich source of quotation. And now, finally, our aberration from the history of the Modern Movement is accomplished.

In reassessing the landmarks of the Modern Movement we discover the importance of past formal principles and methods in producing these works of integrity. This leads us to the conclusion that building is 'architecture' only when it posits a recognisable formal integrity within a cultural context. In other words, the productive method of 'architecture' is an operation of transformation employing quotation and supplementation of an established archive of 'architecture'. The history of 'architecture' is punctuated by instances of this paradigmatic transfer, i.e. the manipulation of Renaissance architecture by Mannerists of the sixteenth century, the decorative preoccupations of the nineteenth century eclectics, and finally, the formal manipulation of the contemporary eclectics. And so in 1970 the whole of the history of architecture has become 'fair game' – viable as a source of quotation. At first glance we are confronted by what appears to be the development of a tautology; indistinguishable from a stream of such contained in the anthology of architectural theory: 'architecture' is created only by the quotation of that 'architecture' already incorporated in the cultural codes. Our mode of operation, juxtaposed to the Modern Movement's position of evolution and progress, offers instead a circular procedure of almost infinite phases of quotation succeeding quotation in infinite play, creating in the end an 'architecture'.

Manner/Quotation

If 'architecture' is to be produced by the quotation of an 'architecture' preserved in the archives of history, then the abstraction of that architectural language, its modification, and final rearrangement in a new synthetic structure, become the next important theme for me. In this case, the mode of manipulation, and means of transformation of the specified 'language' (the language often representing a formal system) becomes a key to the structure of my work. Previously, I labelled this process 'manner'. In the early 1970s I found it almost impossible to relate 'manner' to the framework of architectural concepts, obliging me instead to relegate 'manner' as a corollary to formal operatives. 'Manner' perhaps may be better understood in reference to parallel phenomena from the past: the Manneristic manipulation of the code of Italian Renaissance architecture in the sixteenth century and the theory of one of the Russian formalists, Victor Schiklowsky, who defined his concept of 'defamiliarisation' as a mechanism capable of revealing the ordinary object as something at once extraordinary, and among others; the interpretation of the French novelist, Raymond Roussels by M. Foucault concerning something which Roussels chose to call 'procede'. Roussels's concept of 'procede' is similar in many respects to my concept of 'manner'.

For me the submission of 'manner' to the auxiliary position of a corollary to formal operatives would only affirm a further alienation from Modern architecture – the fruits of an industrial society. I had no preconceptions as to the procedure 'manner' might stimulate. I relied entirely on an instinctive premonition, which led me to concentrate on that key notion which would provide a springboard for the spirit thoroughly immersed in the orthodoxy of Modern architecture. In my early works I used 'manner' obsessively to systematically manipulate primary geometrics. I called this the seven types of manner. This, however, was an unnecessary constraint on 'manner'. It became increasingly certain that I must generalise the scope of this corollary of formal operations. To modify the specific architectural form-system, and to transform it beyond circumstances, became an additional aim of 'manner'. In projecting cubes, mediating these forms by overlapping the proto-typical Palladian ocular motif, in further distorting that space conception by employing the highly polished and reflective surfaces of marble, in once again increasing the ambiguity of space by the endless repetition of squares, 'manner' is exercised.

Quotation thus becomes a necessary adjunct to 'manner'. Moreover, quotation is a means of abstraction and then displacement. Finally, the 'manner' mediated this entire operation. While the 'manner' is an operational process of remarkable complexity, it nevertheless registers the imprint of the individual architect. It is, after all, directed by the thoughts, tastes and hand of the architect. Necessarily, this operation of quotation becomes systemised, as in the Neo-Classical or eclectic periods, thereby reducing the arbitrariness associated with the 'manner'. When, on the contrary, the rules of combination are not established, and the number and progression of images quoted are not fixed, the specific character of the 'manner' is of crucial importance. 'Manner', then, is forced to adopt a rhetoric of its own if it is to function as an autonomous mechanism.

Rhetoric/Metaphor

For example, 'manner' operates rhetorically when a particular system is repeated obsessively, or when the balance of the established order is upset intentionally, or when the nature of an object is intentionally distorted to its limit. This reshuffling of selected architectural elements produces more than a response to artistic statement, it further dictates for those elements a revaluation, namely, a means of criticising 'architecture' itself, if only through the logic inherent in 'architecture'. This rhetoric is nothing but so-called meta-criticism. It is my intention to investigate the transformational process from both an operational and formal perspective. And this can be facilitated by what I call 'rhetorical manner'.

'Architecture', through a series of mechanisms, generates meaning. 'Rhetorical manner' regulates the operation of those mechanisms. Architectural expression is subtle, its symbolic character is often rendered tactilely. We can offer certain forms that possess inherent formal structures which evoke set images. Meaning does persist, the experience of building reveals that this prior knowledge, and experience of architecture eases this process of interpretation. In this respect, architectural expression differs from spoken language. Clarity or the co-ordination of meanings signified to signifier, the objective of verbal codes, does not predominate. Frequently in architecture elements do not signify one meaning. Even when past forms are interspersed, the code broken, and the meaning understood, those forms repossessed and used in a new context will elude interpretation. For these past forms, so transformed, possess new meaning generated by this process of quotation, displacement, and rearrangement. In other words, meaning in 'architecture' is not denotive, but largely connotive. Hence this connoted meaning is grounded in allusion or metaphor. Architecture that speaks – that 'architecture parlante' – calls forth associations. When the quotations enlisted are clear, the source of quotation and associative meaning are made accessible. So too, when the composition is figurative, for example allusions are made to the human face, an erotic curve, shells, trees, the associations constructed will be easily understood.

In most of my work, however, the co-ordination of association is further complicated. The images I fix on are not concrete, and are thus difficult to allude to. Often my work is concerned with natural phenomenon, such as 'twilight', 'cloud', 'water', 'darkness', etc. These images cannot be adequately represented by concrete ornaments or formal graphics. Only by resorting to a different level of communication, or a more abstract means, can such images be appreciated.

Clearly then the rhetorical manner advocates the generation of metaphor. And while these metaphors are only part of the production of that manner, they will inevitably dominate the finished product.

Biographical Notes

1931	Born at Oita on 23rd July Isozaki's father developed the family business of purchasing and transporting of rice into a successful transport enterprise and served as president of the Oita Chamber of Commerce and Industry. In addition, he was the leading member of the 'Amano-gawa' (Milky Way) group of *haiku* poets in Kyushu. Isozaki is the eldest of four children.
1950	Graduated from Oita Ueno-ga-oka High School and commenced study at the University of Tokyo.
1953	Entered Kenzo Tange's seminar in the Architecture Department of the University of Tokyo and submitted diploma thesis to Tange.
1959	Graduated from the Architecture Department of the University of Tokyo. Bachelor's thesis entitled: 'Development of Skyscraper Designs in the USA, 1875–1935'.
1954–63	Member of Kenzo Tange's team and URTEC (1961). Isozaki participated in the development of almost all the works from Tange's studio during this time, however, his contribution was greatest for the Kagawa Prefectural Hall, Imabari City Hall and the Tokyo Plan. Isozaki's influence is apparent in the Yamanashi Communication Centre which was completed after he had left the studio.
1956	Master of Architecture from the University of Tokyo. Thesis entitled, 'Space Concept in the Modern Movement'.
1960	Married Haruko, divorced 1963.
1961	Commenced Doctorate in Architecture at the University of Tokyo.
1963	Established Arata Isozaki Atelier, Tokyo.
1964	Lecturer, Urban Engineering Faculty of Tokyo University.
1965	Participated in the Skopje Reconstruction Plan with Tange and URTEC.
1967	Married Noriko, divorced 1971, two sons, Chu and Kan. Engaged as Chief Architect for Expo '70, Osaka Plan, and Festival Plaza Project.
1969	Moved his architectural practice from Tokyo to Fukuoka in Kyushu.
1970	Artistic crisis brought on by his involvement in the students' movement which protested against the wholesale industrialization of Japanese life.
1972	Re-established Tokyo practice.
1973	Married Aiko Miyawaki, sculptor. Aiko's association with such prominent

innovators of Modern Art as Hans Richter, Marcel Duchamp, Frederick Kiesler and Man Ray was an important factor in his subsequent work. Prior to this (1960) Isozaki had been attracted to the Tokyo Neo-Dadaists whose *avant-garde* activities increased after the ending of the Second World War.

Collaborators (1963–80)

Yasuhiko Yamamato	1963–76
Kijo Rokkaku	1964–8
Noriyuki Miura	1966–74
Shuichi Fujie	1967–
Hiroshi Nishioka	1970–
Takashi Ito	1971–
Hiroshi Aoki	1975–
Yoshio Tsukio	1967–70

List of Works

Executed works are distinguished by **bold** type

1959–60	**Oita Medical Hall, Niage-cho Oita, Oita Prefecture.**
1960	Tokyo Plan 1960 as a member of the Kenzo Tange team.
1960–62	City in the Air sketches I to IV.
1960–62	Ruin – Future City.
1961	Project for Peugeot Building, France.
1962	Joint Core Project.
1964	**Nakayama House and Clinic, Oita, Oita Prefecture.**
1963–4	**Iwata Girls' High School, 1 Iwata-cho, Oita, Oita Prefecture.**
1962–6	**Oita Prefectural Library, Niage-cho, Oita, Oita Prefecture.**
1965–6	Skopje Reconstruction Plan, as a member of the Kenzo Tange team.
1966–7	**Oita branch, Fukuoka Mutual Bank, Chuo-cho, Oita, Oita Prefecture.**
1966–70	Site planning for Expo '70.
1968–9	A's Residence.
1968	**Electric Labyrinth for 14th Triennale, Milan.**
1967–70	**Daimyo branch, Fukuoka Mutual Bank.**
1967–70	**Festival Plaza, Expo '70, Suita, Osaka Urban Prefecture.** Basic concept for space and mechanical equipment.
1970–72	Computer Aided City.
1968–71	**Headquarters, Fukuoka Mutual Bank, Fukuoka, Fukuoka Prefecture.**
1970–71	**Tokyo branch, Fukuoka Mutual Bank, Tokyo.**
1971	**Nagasumi branch, Fukuoka Mutual Bank.**
1971–2	**Ropponmatsu branch, Fukuoka Mutual Bank, Chuo-ku, Fukuoka, Fukuoka Prefecture.**
1972	Operation 'Vesuvius'.
1970–72	**Oita Medical Hall Annex, Niage-cho, Oita, Oita Prefecture.**
1973	**Saga branch, Fukuoka Mutual Bank, Saga Prefecture.**
1971–4	**Gunma Prefectural Museum of Modern Art. Takasaki, Gunma Prefecture.**
1972–4	**Kitakyushu City Museum of Art, Kitakyushu, Fukuoka Prefecture.**

1972–4	**Fujimi Country Clubhouse, Oita, Oita Prefecture.**
1972–5	**Kitakyushu Municipal Central Library, Kokura-kita-cho, Kitakyushu, Fukuoka Prefecture.**
1974–5	**Shukosha Building, Fukuoka, Fukuoka Prefecture.**
1975	**Yano Residence, Kawasaki (outskirts of Tokyo), Kanagawa Prefecture.**
1973–4	Katsuyama Country Clubhouse.
1975	Kawarayu SPA Town.
1975–6	**'Angel Cage and Gravity Room', Opening Show, National Design Museum, New York.**
1975–7	**Kitakyushu Municipal Exhibition Hall, Kitakyushu, Fukuoka Prefecture.**
1978	**Kamioka Town Hall, Kamioka, Gifu Prefecture.**
1977–8	**Oita Audio-Visual Centre, Oita, Oita Prefecture.**
1978	**Sueoka Medical Clinic, Iwata-Nachi, Oita, Oita Prefecture.**
1978	**Kaijima House.**
1978	A Women's College.
1978	Cultural Centre, Japan-Europe.
1978	**Karashima House, Horikawa Street, Chiyomachi 2-chome, Oita, Oita Prefecture.**
1978	**Hayashi House**
1978	Kubo House 1
	Kubo House 2
1978	**Tomb of Don Francisco Sorin Otomo.**
1978	Ao Residence.
1978–80	**Nippon Electric Glass Co., Ltd., Employees' Service Facilities, Ootsu, Shiga Prefecture.**
1979–82	**Tsukuba Civic Centre Project, Tsukuba Academic New Town, Ibaragi Prefecture.**

Exhibitions

1965	Movie Stage Design for 'The Other Man's Face'.
1966	'Space and Color' Exhibition (Tokyo).
1966	'From Space towards Environment', display (Tokyo).
1968	14th Triennale, *Electric Labyrinth* (Milano).
1972	'Operations Vesuvius' (Napoli).
1975	International Exhibition of International Architecture, TERRA-1 (Poland).
1976	One-man Show 'Arata Isozaki Retrospective' (London).
1976	Venezia Biennale 1976, layout of the Japanese Section.
1976	Dortmunder Architecturausstellung.
1976–7	'Man TransForms', opening show of Copper-Hewitt Museum of Design, *Angel Cage & Gravity Room* (New York).
1977–8	One-man Show 'Architecture of Quotation and Metaphor' (Tokyo, Chicago, Lodz).
1977	'Assenza/Presenza' Architectural Exhibition (Bolonga).
1977	Sao Paulo Biennale, art work *The Cubic Frames as a Metaphor for the Museum I & II*.

1977–80	'Numerals; Mathematical Concepts in Contemporary Art' (USA).
1978	'A New Wave of Japanese Architecture' Exhibition throughout U.S.A., participant.
1978–9	Festival D'Automne à Paris 1978; *MA Espace-Temps Au Japon*, concepturizer and designer.
1979·80	*Space-Time in Japan MA* Exhibition in USA (New York, Houston, Chicago).
1980	*Space-Time in Japan MA* Exhibition in Europe (Stockholm).
1980	'City Segments' Architectural Exhibition (USA).
1980	'The Presence of the Past', the First International Exhibition of Architecture at La Biennale di Venezia 'Facade'.
1980	'Architecture II; Houses for Sale' Exhibition at Leo Castelli, New York.

Notes

Chapter 1

1. The essence of populism is that you give the people what they want: or rather you give them literally what they are expressing in their own imagery. It has always been an urgent necessity in America to filter the popular voice through cultural institutions, in place of the social habits which filter it at an earlier stage in Japan and Europe. In his writings and architecture Robert Venturi sought to combine the aesthetic extremes of main street America with the high style of the Renaissance and Mannerism. Charles Jencks has followed, in the main, Venturi's lead, thus in his introduction to *The Language of Post-Modern Architecture* (1978), 8, he explains 'Modern architecture suffered from elitism. Post Modernism is trying to get over the elitism not by dropping it, but rather by extending the language of architecture in many ways – into vernacular, towards tradition and the commercial slang of the street. Hence the doublecoding, the architecture which speaks to the elite and the man on the street'.

2. Muramatsu, T. (June, 1965) 'The Course of Modern Japanese Architecture'. *The Japan Architect* **40**, 6, (109) 45. According to Muramatsu, in the late nineteenth century Japanese architects. . . 'sought to acquire the material substance, the techniques, of Western culture, because in that lay the 'power'. Eclectic styles were a source of study because they contained a necessary concentration of techniques'.

3. Leech, G. (1974) *Semantics*. Harmondsworth, Middlesex: Penguin Books, 45.

4. Leech makes the point that any explanation of linguistic phenomena in terms of what is not language is invalid and suggests instead that linguists should study relations within language. *ibid*, 5.

5. Pevsner, N. (1968). 'The Return to Historicism'. *Studies in Art, Architecture and Design*. **2**, 258.

6. *ibid*, 244.

7. The continuity between Renaissance, Baroque, Rococo, and Neo-Classicism was the result of a common basis of forms. Frankl, P. (1968) *Principles of Architectural History: The Four Phases of Architectural Style, 1420–1900*. Translated and edited by J. F. O'Gorman. Cambridge, Mass.: MIT Press, 191.

8. Isozaki, A. (August, 1971) 'James Stirling in Tokyo'. *Architecture and Urbanism* **1** (8), 7.

9. For a more complete discussion of the ideas and influence of the Metabolism Group see Kawazoe, N. (December 1969, January 1970) 'Metabolism' 1, 2. *The Japan Architect* **44**, (12), 101–108 and **45**, (1), 97–101.

10. Isozaki, A. (November 1977) 'A Comparative Study: Bronx Development Centre and Gunma Prefectural Museum of Modern Art'. *Architecture and Urbanism* **52**, 11, (84), 15–17.

11. Paul Frankl was the first to notice the transformation of an assertive skeletal form into a passive stretched skin in his study of post-medieval architecture. Frankl, P. (1968) *Principles of Architectural History* translated and edited by J. F. O'Gorman. Cambridge Mass.: MIT Press, 129–30.

12. *See* Sasaki, H. (June 1965) 'The Development of Modern Architecture in Japan'. *The Japan Architect* **40**, 6, (109), 67.

13. *See* Shinohara, K. (June 1964) 'The Japanese Conception of Space'. *The Japan Architect* **39**, (6), 56–9.

14. Isozaki, A. (January 1972) 'Manner is Everything'. Translated by D. Goodman. *Architecture and Urbanism* **2**, (1), 16.

15. Isozaki, A. (September 1978) 'An Architecture of Quotation and Metaphor'. *Kenchiku Bunka* **33**, (383), 33.

16. From 'Chronological Notes' (April 1976). *Space Design* (140), 101.

17. Isozaki, A. (April 1976) 'From Manner, to Rhetoric, to. . .'. *The Japan Architect* **51**, 4, (230), 67.

18. Isozaki, A. (October–November 1977) 'Nine Quotation Sources'. *The Japan Architect* **52**, (10–11), 21.

19. Frankl, P. (1968) *Principles of Architectural History*. Translated and edited by J. F. O'Gorman. Cambridge Mass.: MIT Press, 190.

20. Isozaki, A. (August 1972) 'About My Method'. *The Japan Architect* **47**, (8) 22.

21. Isozaki, A. (January 1972) 'Manner is Everything'. Translated by D. Goodman. *Architecture and Urbanism* **2**, (1), 15.

22. *ibid*, 16.

Chapter 2

1. Watkin, D. (1977) *Morality and Architecture*. Oxford: Clarendon Press.

2. Frankl, P. (1968) *Principles of Architectural History*. Translated and edited by J. F. O'Gorman. Cambridge, Mass.: MIT Press, 186.

3. For an analysis of these historical relations see Rowe, C. (1976) *The Mathematics of the Ideal Villa and Other Essays*. Cambridge, Mass: MIT Press.

4. Hauser states that while typologically similar constellations recur in history, identical constellations do not. And even though there has been no recurrence or direct continuation of Mannerism after its end in the seventeenth century, it has survived as an undercurrent in the history of Western art, sometimes more apparent and sometimes less. Hauser, A. (1965) *Mannerism: The Crisis of the Renaissance and the Origin of Modern Art*. London: Routledge and Kegan Paul, **1**, 355.

5. *ibid*.

6. Shearman, J. (1967) *Mannerism*. Harmondsworth, Middlesex: Penguin Books.

7. Hauser, A. (1965) *Mannerism*. London: Routledge & Kegan Paul, **1**, 13.

8. *ibid*, 12.

9. Shearman, J. (1967) *Mannerism*. Harmondsworth, Middlesex: Penguin Books, 171.

10. Hauser, A. (1965) *Mannerism*. London: Routledge & Kegan Paul, **1**, 294.

11. *ibid*, 111.

12. Venturi, R. (1966) *Complexity and Contradiction in Architecture*. New York: The Museum of Modern Art, 24.

13. Hauser, A. (1965) *Mannerism*. London: Routledge & Kegan Paul, **1**, 12.

14. *ibid*, 25.

15. Venturi, R. (1966) *Complexity and Contradiction in Architecture*. New York: The Museum of Modern Art, 22–3.

16. *ibid*, 26.

17. Hauser, A. (1965) *Mannerism*. London: Routledge & Kegan Paul, **1**, 15.

18. *ibid*, 6.

19. *ibid*, 25.

20. *ibid*, 248.

21. *ibid*, 286.

22. *ibid*, 150.

23. *ibid*, 91.
24. *See* Shearman, J. (1967) *Mannerism*. Harmondsworth, Middlesex: Penguin Books, 17.
25. Hauser, A. (1965) *Mannerism*. London: Routledge & Kegan Paul, **1**, 120.
26. Leech, G. (1974) *Semantics*. Harmondsworth, Middlesex: Penguin Books, 43.
27. Hauser, A. (1965) *Mannerism*. London: Routledge & Kegan Paul, **1**, 294.
28. Leech, G. (1974) *Semantics*. Harmondsworth, Middlesex: Penguin Books, 44.
29. Isozaki, A. (January 1972), 'Manner is Everything'. Translated by D. Goodman. *Architecture and Urbanism* **2**, (1), 16.
30. Isozaki, A. (September 1978) 'An Architecture of Quotation and Metaphor'. *Kenchiku Bunka* **33**, (383), 34.
31. Taki, K. (April 1976) 'World in a Mirror (2)' *The Japan Architect* **51**, 4, (230), 69.
32. Isozaki, A. (January 1972) 'Manner is Everything'. Translated by D. Goodman. *Architecture and Urbanism* **2**, (1), 16.
33. For an account of the sources of Isozaki's metaphors and quotations see (October–November 1977) 'Post-Metabolism' *The Japan Architect* **52**, 10–11, (247), 20–24.
34. Kazuhiro Ishii has observed that 'Isozaki's "darkness", too, must represent the inexplicable, enigmatic aspect of his architecture and the very indeterminate form of an individual's world of idea'. Ishii, K. (April 1976) 'A Guide to the World of Arata Isozaki'. *Space Design* **51**, 4, (140), 21.
35. Isozaki, A. (April 1976) 'Rhetoric of the Cylinder'. *The Japan Architect* **51**, 4, (230), 61.
36. *ibid*.
37. Taki, K. (March 1976) 'World in a Mirror'. *The Japan Architect* **51**, 3, (229), 77.
38. Isozaki, A. (March 1976) 'The Metaphor of the Cube'. *The Japan Architect* **51**, 3, (229), 29.

Chapter 3

1. *See* Nitschke, G. (March 1966) '"Ma" and "Ku", The Japanese concept of "Ma" (Place)'. *Architectural Design* **XXXVI**, (3), 153.
2. Kojiro, Y. (June 1964) 'Posts: The Basis of Japanese Interior Space'. *The Japan Architect* **39**, (6), 45.
3. See Kultermann, U. *ed*. (1970) *Kenzo Tange, 1946–1969*. London: Pall Mall Press, 112–49.
4. Ito, N. (May 1964) 'The Styles of Japanese Architecture'. *The Japan Architect* **39**, (5), 81. Bracket systems according to Ito are a signal of the superhuman.
5. (May 1964) 'Conclusion' *The Japan Architect* **39**, (5), 99.
6. Isozaki, A. (August 1972) *The Japan Architect* **47**, (8), 38.
7. For Isozaki's remarks on the significance of his use of colour in the Oita branch Bank see: Muramatsu, T. (October 1973) 'Dialogue with Arata Isozaki'. 3 *The Japan Architect* **48**, (10), 91–2.
8. Isozaki, A. (August 1972) *The Japan Architect* **47**, (8), 38.
9. *See* Kaufmann, E. (1952) *Three Revolutionary Architects, Boullée, Ledoux, and Le Queu*. Philadelphia: Transactions of the American Philosophical Society **42**, (3), 489.

Chapter 4

1. *See* Kaufmann, E. (1968) *Architecture in the Age of Reason*. New York: Dover, 22–8, for a discussion of Robert Morris's cubism.
2. Kaufmann *ibid*, 212 notes that 'Under the rule of individualism however, you may add or remove as many parts as you like'. It is clear that Durand's idea of the equal importance of the elements results in an additive composition of independent elements, a kind of mechanical composition *ad infinitum*.
3. *ibid*, 20.
4. *ibid*, figure 14. For such men as Robert Morris geometry was a means rather than an end in itself. Goethe designed an Altar of Good Fortune in 1777 in his garden at Weimar consisting of a sphere representing the ever-moving sphere of restless desires mounted on a cubic block signifying immobile virtue.
5. Paul Frankl characterises the first phase of post-medieval architecture from 1420 to 1550

as one in which spatial form is structured in an additive fashion. Frankl, P. (1968) *Principles of Architectural History*. Cambridge, Mass.: MIT Press, 29.

6. Emil Kaufmann defined reverberation as the presentation of one and the same motif in different sizes. Kaufmann E. (1968) *Architecture in the Age of Reason*. New York: Dover, 189.

7. *See* Kaufmann, E. (1952) *Three Revolutionary Architects, Boullée, Ledoux, and Le Queu*. Philadelphia Transactions of the American Philosophical Society **42**, (3), figure 164, 524, figure 188, 531.

8. Isozaki, A. (March 1976) 'Personal Notes on the Cube'. *The Japan Architect* **51**, 3, (229), 25.

9. *See* Kaufmann, E. (1952) *Three Revolutionary Architects, Boullée, Ledoux, and Le Queu*. Philadelphia Transactions of the American Philosophical Society **42**, (3), figure 64, 483.

10. *See ibid*, 501.

11. *See ibid*, figures 184, 185, 531.

12. *See ibid*, figures 186, 187, 531.

13. *See* (January 1972) 'An Architect in Ambivalence'. *Architecture and Urbanism* **2**, (1), 28–31.

14. Hauser recognized the tendency to develop the picture in depth instead of in breadth, and to 'transform a broad canvas into a tunnel boring deeply into the background' as typical of Mannerism. Hauser, A. (1965) *Mannerism*. London: Routledge & Kegan Paul, **1**, 158.

15. Hauser considered that as Mannerism increases its abstraction it becomes increasingly remote from nature. This he observes . . . 'it does so in the most striking and paradoxical fashion in the villa, which now so sharply and rigidly isolates itself from its background, as if to emphasise, not their basic unity, but the irreconcilable antagonism between building and environment, civilization and nature, man and his surroundings'. *ibid*, 383–84.

16. *See* Munz, L. and Künstler, G. (1966) *Adolf Loos, Pioneer of Modern Architecture*. London: Thames and Hudson, 101–110.

17. *ibid*, figure 84, 105.

18. Isozaki offers this explanation of the Shukosha Building (March 1976) 'Personal Notes on the Cube'. *The Japan Architect* **51**, 3, (229), 24.

19. *ibid*, 24.

20. Isozaki confirmed the Tokonoma metaphor in (September 1978) *Kenchiku Bunka* **33**, (383), 48(76).

21. Kaufmann, E. (1952) *Three Revolutionary Architects, Boullée, Ledoux, and Le Queu*. Philadelphia: Transactions of the American Philosophical Society **42**, (3), figures 60, 62, 482.

22. Muramatsu, T. (October 1973) 'Dialogue with Arata Isozaki (3)'. *The Japan Architect* **48**, (10), 95.

23. *See* (July 1977) *Architecture and Urbanism*, (79), 81.

24. Kaufmann, E. (1952) *Three Revolutionary Architects, Boullée, Ledoux, and Le Queu*. Philadelphia: Transactions of the American Philosophical Society **42**, (3), figure 170, 527 and figure 191, 532.

25. Frankl, P. (1968) *Principles of Architectural History*, Mass.: MIT Press 130–131.

26. *See* Kaufmann, E. (1952) *Three Revolutionary Architects, Boullée, Ledoux, and Le Queu*. Philadelphia: Transactions of the American Philosophical Society **42**, (3), figure 174, 528.

27. David Wild pointed out the similarity of the Yano Residence and Le Corbusier's schematic interpretation of the Villa Adriana, (Tivoli 1910) as compositions based on interlocking curvilinear forms (January 1977) *Architecture Design* **47**, (1), 38, figure 3.

28. Kaufmann, E. (1952) *Three Revolutionary Architects, Boullée, Ledoux, and Le Queu*. Philadelphia: Transactions of the American Philosophical Society **42**, (3), figure 198, 535.

29. Isozaki, Arata (April 1976) 'Rhetoric of the Cylinder'. *The Japanese Architect* **51**, 4, (230), 61.

30. *ibid*, 62.

31. *See* Kaufmann, E. (1952) *Three Revolutionary Architects, Boullée, Ledoux, and Le Queu*. Philadelphia: Transactions of the American Philosophical Society **42**, (3), 456–468, figure 45, 468.

32. *See* (September 1978) *Kenchiku Bunka* **33**, (383), 52.

Selected Bibliography

Writings on Arata Isozaki

Boyd, R. (1968) 'Arata Isozaki' in *New Directions in Japanese Architecture*. New York: Braziller, 66–71.

Chaitkin, B. (January, 1977) 'Zen and the Art of Arata Isozaki'. *Architectural Design* **47**, (1), 19–20.

Cook, P. (January, 1972) 'Notes on Arata Isozaki'. *Architecture and Urbanism* **2**, (1), 83–4.
(January, 1977) 'Peter Cook on Arata Isozaki'. *Architectural Design* **47**, (1), 30–32.

Herron, R. '"Invisible Architecture" – Japan's Arata Isozaki'. *Lotus 6*. Gruppo Editoriale Electra S.p.A.: Milan.

Hollein, H. (April, 1976) 'Position and Move'. *Space Design* **51**, 4, (140), 4–10.

Ishii, K. (April, 1976) 'A Guide to the World of Arata Isozaki'. *Space Design* **51**, 4, (140), 11–23.

Jencks, C. (March, 1976) 'Isozaki's Paradoxical Cube'. *The Japan Architect* **51**, (3), 47–50.
(January, 1977) 'Arata Isozaki and Radical Eclecticism'. *Architectural Design* **47**, (1), 42–48.

Miller, N. and Cass, H. W. (November, 1979) 'Arata Isozaki: Exploring Form and Experience'. *The American Institute of Architects' Journal* **68**, (13), 44–55.

Miyagawa, A. (March, 1976) 'In the Blank of the Theory of Maniera'. *The Japan Architect* **51**, (3), 21–26.

Muramatsu, T. (October, 1973) 'Humanity and Architecture', dialogue with Arata Isozaki number 3. *The Japan Architect* **48**, (10), 89–96.
(January, 1970) 'Altering the Image of the Architect'. *The Japan Architect* **45**, (1), 102–105.

Taki, K. (March, 1976) 'World in a Mirror' number 1. *The Japan Architect* **51**, (3), 73–8.
(April, 1976) 'World in a Mirror' number 2. *The Japan Architect* **51**, (4), 68–72.

Taylor, J. (September, 1976) 'The Unreal Architecture of Arata Isozaki'. *Progressive Architecture* **LVII**, (9), 72–83.
(August–September, 1977) 'A Visitation from Arata Isozaki'. *Architecture Australia* **66**, (4), 41–4.

Wild, D. (January, 1977) 'Sour Grapes'. *Architectural Design* **47**, (1), 38–40.

Writings by Arata Isozaki

Books

(1971) *Kukan-e* (Collected Writings 1960–9). Tokyo: Bijutsu Shuppan-sha Co. Ltd.

(1975) *Kenchiku-no-kaitai* (Dismantling of Modern Architecture). Tokyo: Bijutsu Shuppan-sha Co. Ltd.

(1976) *Kenchiku Oyobi Kenchikugai-teki Shiko* (dialogue with architects and others). Tokyo: Kajima Institute Publishing Co. Ltd.

(1978) *Kenchiku-no-1930 Nendai* (Architecture in the 1930s). Tokyo: Kajima Institute Publishing Co. Ltd.

(1979) *Shuho-ga* (Collected Writings 1969–78). Tokyo: Bijutsu Shuppan-sha Co. Ltd.

(1979) *Kenchiku-no-Shuji* (notes on a counter architecture). Tokyo: Bijutsu Shuppan-sha Co. Ltd.

(1979) *Kenchiku-no-Chiso* (critical essays on architects, designers and others). Tokyo: Shokoku-sha Publishing Co. Ltd.

(1980) *Abbaye du Thoronet*. Architectural pilgrimage series no. 5. Isozaki with Kishin Shinoyama. Tokyo: Rikuyosha Publishing Co. Ltd.

(1980) *Les Salines Royales de Chaux*. Architectural pilgrimage series no. 10. Isozaki with Kishin Shinoyama. Tokyo: Rikyosha Publishing Co. Ltd.

Articles and Periodicals

(December, 1963) 'Japanese Urban Space'. with Itoh, T., Tsuchida, A. *et al Kenchiku Bunka.*

(July, 1970) 'Directions in Today's Architecture "A discussion between Kenzo Tange and Arata Isozaki".' *The Japan Architect* **45**, (7), 23–8.

(August, 1971) 'James Stirling in Tokyo Interviewed by Arata Isozaki'. *Architecture and Urbanism* **1**, (8), 4–7.

(January, 1972) 'Manner is Everything'. Translated by David Goodman. *Architecture and Urbanism* **2**, (1), 15–18.

(August, 1972) 'About My Method'. *The Japan Architect* Special Feature **47**, (8), 22–8.

(March, 1975) 'Advice from the Judge'. *The Japan Architect* **50**, (3), 20–22.

(February, 1976) 'General Remarks: Thoughts on the Wretched State of Japanese Architectural Education'. *The Japan Architect* **51**, (3), 27–32.

(March, 1976) 'The Metaphor of the Cube'. *The Japan Architect* **51**, (3), 27–32.

(April, 1976) 'From Manner, to Rhetoric, to . . .'. *The Japan Architect* **51**, (4), 64–7.

(April, 1976) 'Rhetoric of the Cylinder'. *The Japan Architect* **51**, (4), 61–3.

(November, 1977) 'A Comparative Study: Bronx Developmental Centre and Gunma Prefectural Museum of Modern Art'. *Architecture and Urbanism* **52**, 11, (84), 15–17.

(September, 1978) 'Architecture of Quotation and Metaphor'. *Kenchiku Bunka*: Special Edition, **33**, (383), 33–48.

(1978) 'City Demolition Industry, Inc.' in 'A New Wave of Japanese Architecture'. New York: *AIUS Catalogue* 10.

(January, 1979) 'Formalism'. *The Japan Architect* **54**, (1), 9–11.

Documentation of Works

(April, 1967) 'Arata Isozaki, Architect and Urban Designer': Works 1965–6'. *The Kentiku* 62–130.

(January, 1972) 'An Architect in Ambivalence'. *Architecture and Urbanism* **2**, (1), 15–92.

(January, 1972) 'Tokyo branch of the Fukuoka Sogo Bank' *The Japan Architect* **47**, (1), 33–40.

(August, 1972) 'Special Feature: Recent Work by Arata Isozaki'. *The Japan Architect* **47**, (8), 21–76.

(March, 1976) 'Arata Isozaki' Special Edition: 'Square, Cube, and Rectangle' number 1. *The Japan Architect* **51**, (3), 19–78.

(April, 1976) 'Arata Isozaki' Special Edition: 'Cylinder and Semicylinder' number 2. *The Japan Architect* **51**, (4), 19–82.

(April, 1976) 'Arata Isozaki' Special Issue. *Space Design* (140), 3–188.

(January, 1977) 'Arata Isozaki' AD Profiles, *Architectural Design* **47**, (1), 19–50.

(March, 1978) 'West Japan: General Exhibition Centre'. *The Japan Architect* **53**, (3), 9–23.

(September, 1978) 'The Latest Works of Arata Isozaki'. Special Edition, *Kenchiku Bunka*. **33**, (383), 29–159.

Isozaki, A. (1978) 'Japanese Time-Space Concept' in *MA Espace-Temps du Japon Paris*: exhibition catalogue Musée des Arts Décoratifs, Festival d'Automme a Paris.

(January, 1979) 'Works: Kamioka Town Hall, H. Residence, K. J. Residence' *The Japan Architect* **54**, (1), 8–37.

Index

Figures in *italics* refer to illustration numbers.